sweet
-and-
TART

sweet
-and-
TART

70 **IRRESISTIBLE RECIPES WITH CITRUS**

CARLA SNYDER

PHOTOGRAPHS BY
NICOLE FRANZEN

CHRONICLE BOOKS
SAN FRANCISCO

Dedication
✳ ✳ ✳

To my mother, Linda Lou Ella Paul Ferguson, who indulged me with
citrus jelly fruit slices on shopping trips, offered sharp advice about
making the most of what you have, and warned that sour thoughts
make wrinkles. Thanks, Mom, for a Sweet Tart life.

And to my granddaughters, Kyley Sue Snyder and Emma Quinn Snyder
. . . we have lots of baking to do.

Library of Congress Cataloging-in-Publication Data available.
ISBN 978-1-4521-3479-6

Manufactured in China

Designed by Vanessa Dina
Illustration by Agnes Lee
Prop styling by Kate Jordan
Food styling by Chelsea Zimmer
Typesetting by Frank Brayton

10 9 8 7 6 5 4 3

Chronicle Books LLC
680 Second Street
San Francisco, California 94107
www.chroniclebooks.com

I always say, when life gives you lemons, make dessert.

Tart and tantalizing, the sharp tang of beloved, bright yellow lemons can't be beaten for both pleasing palates and helping all the flavors of a homemade creation to pop. There's no end to the versatility of lemons—they flavor the airiest cakes, richest ice creams, and iciest sorbets. And for lemon lovers looking for savory renditions, lemon lifts the frothiest soufflés and adds sparkle to crackers and herb muffins. Welcome to *Sweet and Tart,* where you'll find all your favorite citrus desserts, like Mile-High Lemon Meringue Pie and Heavenly Lemon Squares; updated classics, like Limoncello Shortcakes with Berries and Meyer Lemon Ice Cream, and Cara Cara Cheesecake with Chocolate Crust; and sublime savories such as Flat Bread with Lemony Pesto and Ricotta and Marinated Olives with Lemon and Rosemary. To plump up the citrus power, there are also recipes showcasing orange, grapefruit, and lime.

Sweet and Tart is a book for bakers of every level, but with the understanding that work and family schedules are busier than ever. The recipes are straightforward, with start-to-finish and hands-on times, basic equipment (no fancy pans or gadgets), and "zesty" tips for ingredients and techniques. These professional tips are small things, but they really add up to a more enjoyable baking experience, and give you the confidence and information you need to execute a recipe within your time frame and expertise. I also include make-ahead information for those recipes that can be prepared in advance, because knowing you can make a fabulous dish ahead of time can be a wonderful thing.

I love the zing that citrus brings to meals and the fact that sweet-tart flavor is so simple to achieve; all it takes is a zest and a squeeze. Thus this book begins with "A Zest and a Squeeze: Tips, Tools, and Techniques," discussing how to best zest and juice citrus, baking tips, and must-have tools such as Microplanes and reamers.

You'll find something here for everyone who has a taste for citrus, presented in six chapters, each devoted to a different type of pastry or meal occasion—from Lemon Cake with Lemon-Mascarpone Frosting to Orange Sherbet, and from Lemony Blueberry Muffins with Lemon Streusel to Summer Tart with Lemon and Sun-Dried Tomatoes. You'll also find within the Basics chapter all the little extras that make lemon desserts sing, such as lemon and orange curds, lemon marmalade, and candied citrus peel dipped in chocolate. You'll love how these tangy accompaniments ramp up your desserts and add a hint of flavor to otherwise plain confections. For example, a dollop of lemon curd alongside good ol' strawberry shortcake elevates that dessert to another level. Or a slice or two of candied lemon peel is just the thing to go along with an after-dinner espresso. These may seem like luxuries, but actually they are super-easy staples that make life taste sunny.

When it comes to desserts, the punch of lemon is hard to beat. All it takes to get your groove on is a bag of gorgeous citrus fruit from your local market and a few moments to thumb through *Sweet and Tart*, where you'll be sure to find the perfect lemon sweet or snack for any season, occasion, or time frame. So pucker up! Every day is a good day when it includes a delicious citrus delight.

pucker up

Always zest citrus fruit before squeezing. It's so much easier.

When zesting, use organic citrus, or wash the fruit really well to remove pesticides and wax.

Room-temperature citrus yields the most juice. If you store lemons in the refrigerator, warm them up in the microwave for 30 seconds or let the fruit stand at room temperature for at least 1 hour before juicing.

An average lemon yields 3 to 4 Tbsp juice and about 1 Tbsp zest. A lime will yield 1 to 2 Tbsp juice and 1 to 2 tsp zest. An orange will yield ⅓ to ½ cup [80 to 120 ml] juice and 1½ Tbsp zest.

Fine- and **medium-mesh strainers** are handy when separating the seeds and pulp from citrus juice.

Heat-proof spatulas in various sizes are indispensable, and are by far the best tool for stirring lemon curd while it thickens. The flat surface slides across the bottom of the pan, ensuring even cooking and fewer lumps. A round wooden spoon works fine, but if you find one with a flat edge, buy it. You'll love how it stirs things up.

Heavy-duty baking sheets will change your world. They won't torque in the oven once they heat up, which is a fine thing. Buy two for sure, but if you have storage space, four would be ideal.

An **instant-read thermometer** is a great tool for baking as well as for cooking. Use it to check for when breads and rolls are done. Insert the thermometer into the center of a loaf or bun; when it reads 200°F [95°C], the bread is ready.

A **Microplane zester** may be the best tool you ever buy. It effort-lessly takes just the peel from a citrus fruit, and not the bitter white pith that lies underneath. I promise you will never be sorry to give it space in your gadget drawer.

A few **natural-bristle pastry brushes** will come in handy. I'm not a fan of silicone brushes, but that might just be my preference. It's

nice to have a wide brush (about 3 in [7.5 cm]) and a narrower one (2 in [5 cm]) for brushing egg glazes on pastry. Brushes are also great for greasing cake pans. They do a much more thorough job than a piece of butter on paper rubbed into the bottom and sides of a pan. A brush deposits that nonstick grease in the corners, where you really need it.

Buy an inexpensive **oven thermometer** to check the accuracy of your oven. If your oven is off by more than 25°F [5°C], you aren't getting the best performance from it.

Ramekins and other small containers are handy for organizing your ingredients before you bake, as are an assortment of light-weight and heat-proof **stainless-steel bowls**.

I love my stash of vintage bakeware, but sometimes I need a good **springform pan** or a **fluted tart pan with a removable rim**. The newer cake pans are deeper than the pans of yesteryear, making batter spillover a thing of the past. Their heavier gauge insulates and allows baked goods to cook more evenly, without hot spots on the sides or undercooked centers.

If you love to bake, invest in a **stand mixer**. You will never be sorry. It's lovely to be able to walk away from the mixer and continue to prep ingredients while the butter and sugar are beating up light and fluffy or your bread dough is kneading. In addition, a stand mixer is more powerful than a handheld one and will save you time, since it beats up egg whites and sugar-butter combinations efficiently and quickly.

Trigger ice-cream scoops are great for scooping muffin and cupcake batters into tins, and smaller scoops specifically made for cookie dough will really speed things up for you in the kitchen. I use scoops in these sizes: 3 Tbsp, 1 Tbsp, and ½ Tbsp.

sweet
and tart

Whisks in a few sizes are helpful, but if you have space for only one, make it a big one, since the wider basket works most effectively to incorporate dry ingredients before mixing, and swishes through eggs and other liquids to blend and emulsify them.

A **wooden reamer** is also useful. Lots of tools help you squeeze the juice from citrus efficiently, but this gadget may be the best. Or, in a pinch, try a low-tech fork—stick the tines in the cut lemon and squeeze while twisting the fork.

✻ ✻ ✻

Use **cane sugar**. While working in a bakery, I discovered that cane sugar performs best. Some granulated sugar is derived from beets and will respond a little differently than cane sugar in baking.

I like **kosher salt** and use it when baking. Diamond Crystal is my favorite brand, but Morton will do. Regular iodized table salt has so many additives that it leaves a metallic taste in your mouth . . . and in your food.

Use **large eggs**. Other sizes will throw off the ratios of other ingredients and you won't get the best results. To break eggs cleanly, rap them gently on the counter and separate the two sides of the shell. Breaking them on the edge of a bowl can drive the shell into the egg and often breaks the yolk. When separating eggs, try to break the shell in half as cleanly as possible, and use the shell to pass the yolk back and forth, allowing the whites to fall into a clean bowl. Separate eggs one at a time into a small bowl, and then transfer each clean white to a larger bowl. If you break a yolk in the small bowl, you can just toss it out; any fat in the yolks will prevent the whites from whipping up. By keeping the whites yolk-free, you have a better chance of achieving a fluffy meringue. Eggs separate more easily when cold, but for the best meringues, try to allow time for the whites to warm up to room temperature before whipping.

Overwhipped whites will look a little curdled and grainy. They're more collapsible than underbeaten whites, so it's always preferable to underwhip slightly than to overwhip. Just whip until firm peaks form but the whites are still smooth on the surface. That way, they'll hold up better when folded into other ingredients, retaining more air bubbles, and will yield an airier soufflé, cake, or mousse.

If you have any concerns about eating raw eggs, use pasteurized eggs in recipes in which the eggs are not fully cooked.

Use **pure vanilla extract**. It makes a world of difference. I use Nielsen-Massey vanilla, but any pure extract will suffice. The same is true for lemon, orange, and almond extracts as well as lemon oil and orange oil.

I use **unbleached all-purpose flour**. It's a little healthier and, heaven knows, when you're eating all these desserts, a little healthier can mean a lot.

I use **unsalted butter** because it's a fresher product. Salt is added to butter to give it a longer shelf life. When baking, add your own salt as directed in the recipe.

It's a splurge to buy **vanilla beans,** but you can use them again after removing the seeds. The flavor won't be as strong the second time around, but there's still lots of flavor going on in that leathery pod. To reuse them, simply rinse and dry the pods, then (1) nestle in 2 cups [400 g] granulated sugar to flavor it for a topping on sugar cookies, (2) plunge into a bottle of vodka and add more pods as you have them to use as a form of vanilla extract after the vodka turns a caramel brown, (3) add to mulled ciders, or (4) add to simple syrups for cocktails.

sweet
and tart

When you need softened butter or cream cheese for a recipe but didn't take it out of the fridge ahead of time, here's what to do: Unwrap the butter or cheese and place on a plate. Microwave on full power for 11 seconds. Press with your finger to see how soft it is; you should be able to press and make an indentation. Then turn the sticks or block over and microwave for another 11 seconds. Repeat, if necessary, microwaving for shorter periods.

In baking, weighing ingredients is always the most precise, but if you don't have a scale and are using the scoop-and-sweep method of measuring flour, be sure to fluff it first and then scoop and level. If it is tightly packed, there will be too much flour in your recipe, resulting in stiff doughs and tough cakes and cookies.

When mixing batters and doughs, stop the mixer occasionally to scrape down the sides of the bowl with a rubber spatula. This will ensure that all the ingredients are properly mixed.

I always preheat my oven 25°F [5°C] hotter than the recipe calls for. That way, when I open the oven door and some of the heat escapes, the oven doesn't have to work as hard to return to temperature. After you place the pan in the oven, be sure to lower the temperature to the correct setting.

Bake cakes and cookies in the center of the oven, and pies and tarts in the lower third. Most ovens have hot spots, so rotate the pans 180 degrees about halfway through the cooking time to ensure even baking. If you're baking more than one pan at a time, also switch the pans between the oven racks halfway through.

CHAPTER 1

BARS AND COOKIES

Now that I think about it, it was probably a simple lemon bar that kicked off my lemon lust eons ago. Tangy, tart, and rich, a nibble of a lemon cookie or bar is the perfect ending to a meal or beginning of a midday snack. International offerings from the Far East (Yujacha Marmalade-Filled Walnut Squares), the tropics (Key Lime Bars with Tropical Nut Crust), Greece (Baklava with Cinnamon and Orange), and Italy (Lemony Ricotta Cookies) alert me to the fact that I'm not the only one crazy about citrus desserts.

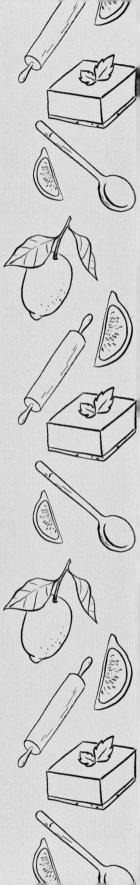

KEY LIME BARS
WITH TROPICAL NUT CRUST

Start to finish:
3 hours, 20 minutes
Hands-on time: 45 minutes

Reminiscent of Key lime pie, these little squares pack a super-limey punch. The gingersnap crust includes almonds and coconut, and makes these bars perfect for your next warm-weather cookout or family get-together.

CRUST

3 cups [300 g] gingersnap cookies

1 cup [120 g] almonds

⅓ cup [65 g] granulated sugar

¼ tsp kosher salt

½ cup [110 g] unsalted butter, melted

1 cup [95 g] sweetened shredded coconut

TOPPING

2 cups [400 g] granulated sugar

¼ cup plus 1 Tbsp [40g] unbleached all-purpose flour

½ cup [110 g] unsalted butter, melted

5 large eggs, beaten lightly

Zest of 2 limes

1 cup [240 ml] bottled Key lime juice

Pinch of kosher salt

Powdered sugar for garnish (optional)

TO MAKE THE CRUST: Preheat the oven to 350°F [180°C]. Line the bottom and sides of a 9-by-13-in [23-by-33-cm] baking pan with aluminum foil, letting the excess hang over the sides of the pan. (The overhang will help you lift the bars from the pan.) Grease the foil.

Put the gingersnaps in the bowl of a food processor and grind to fine crumbs. Transfer the ground cookies to another bowl. Process the almonds, granulated sugar, and salt until finely ground. Add the cookie crumbs to the almond mixture in the processor bowl, then add the melted butter and coconut. Pulse until completely mixed.

Dump the crust mixture into the prepared pan and, using the bottom of a glass or measuring cup, press the mixture to compact and firm it in the bottom of the pan. Bake for 10 minutes, or until the crust is set and golden. Let cool on a wire rack for 20 minutes. Leave the oven on.

sweet and tart

continued

TO MAKE THE TOPPING: Whisk the granulated sugar and flour in a medium bowl, then whisk in the melted butter, eggs, lime zest, Key lime juice, and salt.

Pour the topping over the baked crust and bake for 40 to 45 minutes, or until the topping is set.

Let cool completely in the pan on a wire rack, then cover and refrigerate until fully set, about 2 hours. Loosen the sides with a knife if necessary and lift the bars from the pan using the overhanging foil. Gently turn and peel the foil off the crust (it might stick a little), then turn right-side up and transfer to a cutting board. Cut the bars with a large knife into 2-in [5-cm] squares, wiping the knife clean with a damp paper towel between cuts. Dust with powdered sugar if desired. Store, covered, in the refrigerator for up to 2 days.

MAKES ABOUT THIRTY 2-IN [5-CM] BARS

YUJACHA MARMALADE—FILLED WALNUT SQUARES

3 cups [360 g] chopped walnuts

2 cups [440 g] unsalted butter, softened

2 cups [400 g] sugar

Zest of 2 lemons

2 large eggs

4 cups [480 g] unbleached all-purpose flour

½ tsp kosher salt

2 cups [560 g] *yujacha* marmalade or citron tea (see Zesty Tip)

Start to finish:
2 hours, 30 minutes
Hands-on time: 30 minutes

Preheat the oven to 325°F [165°C]. Line a 9-by-13-in [23-by-33-cm] baking pan with parchment paper.

Spread the walnuts out on a baking sheet and bake for 10 minutes, stirring once. Check to see if they've begun to brown and toast; they should be fragrant. If needed, continue baking for a few minutes more to finish browning. Check frequently, as nuts can overbrown quickly. Let the nuts cool completely.

Beat the butter and sugar in a mixer bowl on high speed until light and fluffy. Beat in the lemon zest and eggs, one at a time, until well combined. Turn the speed to low and beat in the flour, salt, and walnuts until combined.

With lightly floured fingers, press half of the dough into the prepared pan. Spread the marmalade over the dough, leaving a 1-in [2.5-cm] border around the edges. Flatten the remaining dough into pieces with your hands and lay them over the top, leaving open spots (the dough will spread as it bakes). Bake for 1 hour, or until set and browned.

Let cool in the pan on a wire rack for 1 hour, then turn out onto a cutting board and cut into 2-in [5-cm] squares. Store, covered, at room temperature for up to 1 week, or freeze for up to 6 weeks.

MAKES THIRTY 2-IN [5-CM] SQUARES

I've been making these nutty bars for as long as I can remember, swapping out the jammy filling for variety. They were a favorite treat for the kids on family road trips, picnics, or anytime we needed something delicious that could easily be eaten out of hand. Unlike unruly, car-bound children, these bars travel well, and are a welcome sight on the afternoon, adult coffee-break trail as well. Use almonds, pecans, or hazelnuts instead of walnuts, if you'd like, or explore other marmalades or fruit preserves for the filling.

ZESTY TIP

You can find this heavenly product in Asian markets, often also labeled "citron tea." (A tablespoon of the marmalade-like syrup stirred into hot water is a popular restorative beverage.) Yuja, or yuzu, is a citrus fruit that is a cross between a sour mandarin orange and a lemon, grown mostly in Japan and Korea. It's worth the search for this tart and flavorful marmalade, but you can substitute homemade Lemon Marmalade (page 160) or purchased orange or lemon marmalade.

HEAVENLY LEMON SQUARES

Start to finish: 6 hours
Hands-on time: 25 minutes

Lemon squares just might be the perfect dessert. The epitome of lemon-ness, these small bites are a fine ending to any manner of casual dinner or picnic, or a midday snack on the sly. They're heavenly because the lemon filling, rich with butter and lemon zest, shines atop a firm, easy-to-eat-with-your-fingers crust. They may be most delicious gobbled secretly while leaning over the kitchen sink (to catch the crumbs), then licking your fingers clean. Perfect.

1 cup [220 g] unsalted butter, softened and cut into chunks

1 cup [125 g] almond meal or finely ground almonds

¾ cup [90 g] unbleached all-purpose flour

½ cup [60 g] powdered sugar, plus more for dusting (optional)

¾ tsp kosher salt

4 large eggs

1 cup [200 g] granulated sugar

Zest of 2 lemons, plus ¾ cup [180 ml] fresh lemon juice

Preheat the oven to 350°F [180°C]. Line an 8-in [20-cm] square baking pan with parchment paper, letting the excess hang over the sides of the pan. (The overhang will help you to lift the bars from the pan.)

Beat ½ cup [110 g] of the butter, the almond meal, flour, powdered sugar, and ½ tsp of the salt in a mixer bowl on medium-high speed until the mixture comes together. It will still be crumbly but will hold together when compressed.

Press the dough evenly into the bottom of the prepared baking pan, using the bottom of a glass or measuring cup to help compact it. Bake for 20 to 25 minutes, or until the edges are golden brown. Remove from the oven and let cool. Leave the oven on.

Meanwhile, whisk the eggs, granulated sugar, lemon zest, lemon juice, and remaining ¼ tsp salt in a small saucepan. Add the remaining ½ cup [110 g] butter and cook over medium-high heat, stirring gently but continuously with a heat-proof rubber spatula or wooden spoon, until the butter melts and the mixture thickens and coats the back of the spatula, or registers about 160°F [70°C] on an instant-read thermometer. This should take 5 to 10 minutes,

continued

depending on the size of your pan and the strength of your burners. Watch closely and don't let the mixture boil (it will curdle). Transfer the curd to a bowl and stir for a few minutes to stop the cooking and let it cool slightly.

When the crust is cool, spread the curd over the top. Return to the oven and bake for 10 to 15 minutes, or until the edges of the curd are set but the middle is still wiggly. (The bars will firm up as they chill.)

Let the bars cool completely in the pan on a wire rack, then cover and refrigerate for at least 4 hours, or up to overnight. Lift the bars from the pan using the overhanging parchment paper and transfer to a cutting board. Cut the bars with a large knife into 2-in [5-cm] squares, wiping the knife clean with a damp paper towel between cuts. Dust with powdered sugar, if desired. Store, covered, in the refrigerator for up to 3 days.

MAKES SIXTEEN 2-IN [5-CM] SQUARES

MEYER LEMON DROP COOKIES

3 cups [360 g] unbleached all-purpose flour

2 tsp baking powder

1 tsp kosher salt

¾ cup [170 g] unsalted butter, softened

1½ cups [300 g] granulated sugar

Zest of 3 Meyer lemons; plus ¼ cup [60 ml] fresh Meyer lemon juice, plus 3 Tbsp

1 tsp lemon extract

3 large eggs

2 cups [240 g] powdered sugar

Start to finish: 1 hour
Hands-on time: 20 minutes

Sometimes a soft, pillowy cookie is just the ticket to happiness. Especially a lemon bomb like these Meyer lemon–infused cookies. It's a treat that every kid (and adult) would love to find in their lunchbox.

Preheat the oven to 375°F [190°C]. Line two baking sheets with parchment paper.

Whisk the flour, baking powder, and salt in a medium bowl until combined. Set aside.

Beat the butter, granulated sugar, and two-thirds of the lemon zest in a mixer bowl on medium-high speed until light and fluffy. Beat in the ¼ cup [60 ml] lemon juice and the lemon extract and then the eggs, one at a time. Turn the speed to low and beat in the flour mixture in three additions just until combined.

Drop the dough by tablespoons or use a 1-Tbsp scoop to scoop the dough onto the prepared baking sheets, spacing them about 2 in [5 cm] apart. Bake for about 20 minutes, or until just firm to the touch, rotating the baking sheets 180 degrees about halfway through the baking time.

continued

bars and cookies

Let cool on the baking sheets on wire racks for 10 minutes, then lift the cookies from the parchment with a spatula and let cool completely on the racks. Repeat to bake the remaining dough on the same sheets.

Combine the powdered sugar, 3 Tbsp lemon juice, and remaining lemon zest in a small bowl and blend with a fork to make a glaze. (If the glaze is too thick to drizzle, add a few drops of lemon juice or water.)

Set the wire racks over a baking sheet and drizzle the glaze over the cooled cookies with a fork. (The sheet will catch the drips, which can be scraped up and reused if you run short of glaze.) Let set for 20 minutes. Store, covered, at room temperature for up to 5 days, or freeze for up to 6 weeks.

MAKES ABOUT 60 COOKIES

sweet
and tart

LEMONY RICOTTA COOKIES

Start to finish: 2 hours
Hands-on time: 30 minutes

Italian cookies are some of the best in the world, and these lemony rounds are perfect for a tea tray or to go with that afternoon wake-me-up coffee following a siesta. The ricotta cheese makes them moist and fluffy, almost kind of cheesecakey, and the lemon glaze adds a tart finishing touch. Nonna would definitely approve.

3 cups [360 g] unbleached all-purpose flour

1 tsp baking powder

1 tsp kosher salt

½ cup [110 g] unsalted butter, softened

2 cups [400 g] granulated sugar

2 large eggs, at room temperature

One 15-oz [425-g] container whole-milk ricotta cheese

Zest of 2 lemons, plus 5 Tbsp fresh lemon juice

1 tsp lemon oil

½ tsp vanilla extract

1½ cups [180 g] powdered sugar

Preheat the oven to 350°F [180°C]. Line two baking sheets with parchment paper.

Whisk the flour, baking powder, and salt in a medium bowl until combined. Set aside.

Beat the butter and granulated sugar in a mixer bowl on medium-high speed until fluffy. Add the eggs, one at a time, scraping down the sides of the bowl if necessary. Add the ricotta, half of the lemon zest, 2 Tbsp of the lemon juice, the lemon oil, and vanilla and beat until well combined. Turn the speed to low and add the flour mixture in three additions, mixing just until blended and scraping down the sides of the bowl as necessary.

Use a 2-Tbsp scoop to scoop the dough onto the prepared baking sheets, about 12 cookies per sheet, spacing them about 2 in [5 cm] apart. They will spread a little bit. Bake for about 22 minutes, or until puffy and firm, rotating the baking sheets 180 degrees about halfway through the baking time.

Let cool completely on the baking sheets on wire racks, then lift the cookies from the parchment with a spatula. Repeat to bake the remaining dough on the same sheets.

Combine the powdered sugar, remaining lemon zest, and remaining 3 Tbsp lemon juice in a medium bowl and blend with a fork to make a glaze.

Dip the top half of the cooled cookies into the glaze and return to the parchment-lined sheets to dry and set, about 1 hour. (If the glaze is too thick and won't adhere to the cookies, add a few drops of water.) Store, covered, at room temperature for up to 3 days, or freeze for up to 3 months.

MAKES ABOUT 48 COOKIES

LEMON SHORTBREAD
WITH LEMON GLAZE

Start to finish: 4 hours
Hands-on time: 1 hour

Lemon shortbread just might be my favorite cookie ever. It has the richness to satisfy without being overly sweet or cloying. At the Great Lakes Bakery, where I used to work, we baked with an eye to saving time, so we rolled the dough into a log and refrigerated it, then sliced the cookies before baking them off. It's so much easier than rolling out the dough and cutting the cookies out with a cutter; plus you get the bonus of the crunchy sugar around the edges. Saves time and you get a tastier cookie—what could be better?

ZESTY TIP

If you want to keep the log of dough to bake off cookies at a later date, store it chilled in the fridge for up to 2 days, or freeze portions for up to 1 month and thaw them in the fridge for a few hours before slicing.

1 cup [220 g] unsalted butter, softened

1½ cups [180 g] powdered sugar

Zest of 3 lemons, plus 2 Tbsp fresh lemon juice

Pinch of kosher salt

1 tsp vanilla extract

2½ cups [300 g] unbleached all-purpose flour

1 egg white, beaten

⅓ cup [65 g] turbinado or raw sugar

Beat the butter, ¾ cup [90 g] of the powdered sugar, three-fourths of the lemon zest, and the salt in a mixer bowl on medium-high speed until light and fluffy, about 2 minutes. Turn the speed to low and add the vanilla, then the flour in 1-cup [120-g] increments. The dough should be firm.

Transfer the dough to a work surface and shape into a log, rolling it to a size of about 8 by 2 in [20 by 5 cm]. Center it on a sheet of parchment paper and roll so it is as uniformly round as possible. Enclose the dough in the parchment and refrigerate until firm, about 2 hours.

Preheat the oven to 350°F [180°C]. Line two baking sheets with parchment paper.

Unwrap the log and brush all over with the egg white. Sprinkle the turbinado sugar over the dough and press with your hands to make it adhere, rolling to coat it completely. Cut the log into slices about ¼ in [6 mm] thick and transfer to the prepared baking sheets, spacing them about 2 in [5 cm] apart. Bake for about 17 minutes, or until firm, rotating the baking sheets 180 degrees about halfway through the baking time. The cookies will be pale but lightly golden around the edges.

sweet and tart

Let cool completely on the baking sheets on wire racks.

Combine the remaining ¾ cup [90 g] powdered sugar, the lemon juice, and remaining lemon zest in a small bowl and blend with a fork to make a glaze. (If the glaze is too thick to drizzle, add a few drops of lemon juice or water. If it is too thin, add more powdered sugar.)

Set the wire racks over a baking sheet and drizzle the glaze over the cooled cookies with a fork. (The sheet will catch the drips, which can be scraped up and reused if you run short of glaze.) Let set for about 1 hour. Store, covered, at room temperature for up to 1 week.

MAKES ABOUT 36 COOKIES

GALAKTOBOUREKO

Start to finish:
1 hour, 20 minutes, plus
1 hour for cooling
Hands-on time: 30 minutes

Most people in the United States are familiar with baklava, that nutty, honey-drenched dessert from the Mediterranean. But have you ever tried *galaktoboureko*? It's a sweet custard baked between sheets of buttery phyllo, then drenched in a sweet syrup flavored with lemon, a sort of Greek milk tart. My family devoured every last crumb and clamored for more.

ZESTY TIP

Phyllo dough comes in a 1-lb [455-g] box, packaged in two rolls of about twenty sheets. For this recipe, you'll use one roll plus four sheets of the second. Phyllo dough does not refreeze well; refrigerate remaining opened phyllo, tightly wrapped in plastic, for up to 3 days.

2 cups [480 ml] milk

1 cup [120 g] unbleached all-purpose flour

1 cup [200 g] sugar

5 large eggs

1 tsp vanilla extract

Twenty-four 9-by-14-in [23-by-35.5-cm] sheets frozen phyllo pastry dough (about 10 oz [280 g]), thawed

½ cup [110 g] unsalted butter, melted

LEMON-SCENTED SIMPLE SYRUP

1½ cups [300 g] sugar

1 cup [240 ml] water

2 Tbsp fresh lemon juice

Preheat the oven to 350°F [180°C]. Butter a 9-by-13-in [23-by-33-cm] baking pan.

Whisk the milk, flour, and sugar in a large saucepan until combined. Bring to a simmer over medium heat and cook, stirring, until thickened to the consistency of pudding, about 5 minutes. Remove from the heat and let cool for 5 minutes (it will continue to thicken). Whisk in the eggs, one at a time, followed by the vanilla. Set the custard aside.

Remove the phyllo from its wrapper and cover with a large sheet of plastic wrap topped by a damp dish towel. (Keep the pastry covered when not working with it to prevent air from drying it out.) Trim the phyllo sheets so they will fit in the bottom of the pan without overlapping the sides.

To build the *galaktoboureko*, you will alternate two layers of dough with one layer of custard filling. Start with a base of six sheets of phyllo on the bottom, brushing the top of each sheet with melted butter. Spread the custard evenly over the stacked sheets. Top with another six sheets of phyllo, again brushing the top of each with melted butter.

sweet and tart

If you have the time, cover and refrigerate the *galakto-boureko* for 30 minutes so the butter sets (this will make it easier to cut after baking because the pastry becomes very flaky). Using a sharp knife, cut through the top few layers of the pastry into 3-in [7.5-cm] squares. Bake for about 45 minutes, or until golden and flaky.

MEANWHILE, MAKE THE SIMPLE SYRUP: Combine the sugar and water in a medium saucepan over medium-high heat and bring to a boil, then boil, stirring occasionally, for about 5 minutes, or until the mixture is syrupy. Remove from the heat and stir in the lemon juice.

Remove the *galaktoboureko* from the oven and, follow-ing the cuts already made, cut completely through so the syrup can penetrate all the layers. Pour the syrup evenly over the hot pastry. Let stand for at least 1 hour before serving, so the syrup can seep into all the cuts and spread throughout the dessert. Store, covered, in the refrigerator for up to 2 days.

MAKES EIGHTEEN 3-IN [7.5-CM] SQUARES

BAKLAVA
WITH CINNAMON AND ORANGE

Start to finish: 2 hours, plus
several hours to cool
Hands-on time: 50 minutes

It's sticky and gooey and finger-lickin'
good. My husband and I had the most
amazing baklava on the Greek isle
of Santorini, which then kicked off a
vision quest to re-create this nutty
classic. I remember the distinct flavor
of the honey there and though we can't
source Santorini honey here, I think I've
come pretty close with the addition of
orange peel, cinnamon, and clove to the
syrup. Yum.

3 cups [360 g] walnuts, toasted
(see page 19)

1 cup [120 g] hazelnuts, toasted
and skinned (see Zesty Tip,
page 139)

⅓ cup [65 g] sugar

½ tsp ground cinnamon

¼ tsp ground cloves

Pinch of kosher salt

Twenty-four 9-by-14-in
[23-by-35.5-cm] sheets frozen
phyllo pastry dough (about
10 oz [280 g]), thawed

¾ cup [170 g] unsalted butter,
melted

**ORANGE-SCENTED
SIMPLE SYRUP**

1 cup [200 g] sugar

1 cup [240 ml] water

⅓ cup [110 g] honey

2 large strips orange peel

1 cinnamon stick

2 whole cloves

Preheat the oven to 375°F [190°C]. Butter a 9-by-13-in
[23-by-33-cm] baking pan.

Combine the walnuts, hazelnuts, sugar, cinnamon, ground
cloves, and salt in the bowl of a food processor and pulse
to chop finely. Set aside.

Remove the phyllo from its wrapper and cover with a large
sheet of plastic wrap topped by a damp dish towel. (Keep
the pastry covered when not working with it to prevent air
from drying it out.) Trim the phyllo sheets so they will fit in
the bottom of the pan without overlapping the sides.

To build the baklava, you will alternate three layers of
dough with two layers of nut mixture. Start with a base
of eight sheets of phyllo on the bottom, brushing the top
of each sheet with melted butter. Spread half of the nut
mixture evenly over the stacked sheets and press lightly.
Cover with another four sheets of phyllo, again brushing

sweet
and tart

the top of each with melted butter, then spread with the remaining nut mixture, pressing to compact it slightly. Top with the last eight sheets of phyllo, brushing each with butter the same way.

If you have the time, cover and refrigerate the baklava for 30 minutes so the butter sets (this will make it easier to cut after baking because the pastry becomes very flaky). Using a sharp knife, make six to eight cuts on the diagonal lengthwise through the top few layers of pastry, then cut diagonally from the opposite direction to form 2-in [5-cm] diamonds. Bake for about 40 minutes, or until golden and flaky.

MEANWHILE, MAKE THE SIMPLE SYRUP: Combine the sugar, water, honey, orange peel, cinnamon stick, and whole cloves in a medium saucepan over high heat and bring to a boil. Turn the heat to low and simmer, stirring occasionally, for 10 minutes, or until thickened. Remove and discard the orange peel, cinnamon stick, and cloves. Let cool slightly.

Remove the baklava from the oven and, following the cuts already made, cut completely through so the syrup can penetrate all the layers. Pour the syrup evenly over the hot baklava. Let stand for several hours before serving, so the syrup can seep into all the cuts and spread throughout the dessert. Store, covered, at room temperature for up to 3 days.

MAKES ABOUT THIRTY 2-IN [5-CM] PIECES

ORANGEY FIG AND ALMOND BISCOTTI

Start to finish: 2 hours
Hands-on time: 40 minutes

There's nothing like having a great biscotti recipe in your culinary arsenal. I bake these ahead and freeze them so that I have a light and easy dessert or snack on hand at all times. The figs are a little unusual in biscotti, but they partner well with the orange and will fast become one of your favorite combos.

1½ cups [180 g] slivered almonds

2¾ cups [330 g] unbleached all-purpose flour

1½ tsp baking powder

½ tsp kosher salt

1½ cups [300 g] sugar

½ cup [110 g] unsalted butter, softened

Zest of 3 oranges

2 large eggs

¼ cup [60 ml] Cointreau or other orange-flavored liqueur

1½ cups [255 g] stemmed and quartered dried Mission figs

Preheat the oven to 350°F [180°C]. Line two baking sheets with parchment paper. Set aside.

Spread the almonds out in a small baking pan and bake for 5 minutes, stirring once. Check to see if they've begun to brown and toast; they should be fragrant and golden in color. If needed, continue baking for a few more minutes to finish browning. It's best to check frequently, as nuts can overbrown quickly. Let the nuts cool completely in the pan on a wire rack.

Whisk the flour, baking powder, and salt in a medium bowl until combined. Set aside.

Beat the sugar, butter, and orange zest in a mixer bowl on medium-high speed until mixed well. Add the eggs, one at a time, and beat until blended. Add the Cointreau and beat until combined. Turn the speed to low, add the flour mixture, almonds, and figs, and beat until combined.

continued

sweet and tart

Divide the dough into thirds. Shape each piece into a 10-by-3-in [25-by-7.5-cm] log and place on one of the prepared baking sheets. Bake for about 30 minutes, or until browned but still soft, rotating the baking sheet 180 degrees about halfway through the baking time.

Let cool completely on the baking sheet on a wire rack. Transfer the logs to a cutting board and cut crosswise into ¾-in [2-cm] slices. Return the cookies, cut-side up, to both baking sheets. Lower the oven temperature to 300°F [150°C] and bake for 15 minutes. Turn the cookies over, rotate the baking sheets, and bake for another 10 minutes, or until crispy and somewhat dried.

Let cool completely on the baking sheets on wire racks. Store, covered, at room temperature for up to 2 weeks, or freeze for up to 6 weeks.

MAKES ABOUT 36 BISCOTTI

CHAPTER 2
PASTRIES, COBBLERS, TARTS, AND PIES

Many varieties of fruits love mingling with citrus. It brings out the best and brightest flavor in berries, pears, and nectarines. So it shouldn't be a big surprise to find, nestled in this chapter among the lemon meringue and grapefruit custard pies, a few fruity yet very citrusy pie and tart options, just to keep things interesting.

LEMON CURD NAPOLEONS
WITH RASPBERRIES AND RASPBERRY COULIS

Start to finish: 2 hours
Hands-on time: 40 minutes

Napoleon was a little guy, so I'm not sure why these highly stacked pastries have been so named; perhaps because they pack so much punch in a little package. And there aren't many desserts that are so easy to assemble yet so impressive or commanding. Hmmmm. Napoleon, anyone?

ZESTY TIPS

I've instructed you to use store-bought puff pastry because there are some excellent packaged ones out there. Look for Dufour at specialty markets. It's as close as you can come to homemade quality with store-bought ease.

The puff pastry can be baked a day ahead and kept lightly covered with plastic wrap at room temperature. The coulis can be made up to 4 days ahead; store, covered, in the refrigerator.

One 17.3-oz [490-g] package frozen puff pastry (2 sheets), thawed

3 Tbsp powdered sugar, plus more for garnish

One 10-oz [280-g] package frozen raspberries in syrup, thawed

2 tsp fresh lemon juice

2 cups [560 g] Lemon Curd (page 158)

1½ cups [180 g] fresh raspberries, plus more for garnish

Preheat the oven to 400°F [200°C]. Line a baking sheet with parchment paper.

Cut each sheet of puff pastry into nine squares (eighteen total) and sift the 3 Tbsp powdered sugar on both sides of the squares. Place in a single layer on the prepared baking sheet and lay a greased cooling rack upside down on top of the pastries (this will prevent them from puffing up too much when baking but still allow them to brown). Refrigerate for 20 minutes. Bake for 10 to 12 minutes, or until the pastry is golden and crispy. Immediately remove the rack (some of the pastries might stick a little, but you only need six pretty ones for the tops). Let cool completely.

Combine the frozen raspberries with their syrup and the lemon juice in the bowl of a food processor and blend until smooth. Push the mixture through a fine-mesh strainer into a bowl to remove the seeds, transfer to a squeeze bottle if you have one, and refrigerate for up to 3 days. (Otherwise, refrigerate the raspberry coulis in a covered bowl.)

Place one pastry square on a dessert plate and spread with about 3 Tbsp of the lemon curd. Add a layer of fresh raspberries and then top with another pastry square, more lemon curd, more fresh berries, and a third pastry square. Garnish the plate with a squirt or a splash of raspberry coulis and extra berries, and dust with powdered sugar. Repeat to assemble the remaining napoleons. Serve immediately, or refrigerate for up to 30 minutes (no longer, or the pastry will become soggy).

SERVES 6

pastries,
41 cobblers,
tarts, and
pies

NECTARINE AND BERRY CRISP
WITH LEMON VERBENA

Start to finish: 1 hour, 15 minutes
Hands-on time: 30 minutes

This is my favorite rendition of the classic crisp. I also have an affection for combining plums, peaches, and apricots in this summery dessert, though you must peel the fuzzier fruits before tossing with the berries. My trademark addition is lemon verbena, which I plant every spring without fail. It's lemony like lemongrass but with an herbal green note that I find addictive. But don't let a lack of lemon verbena stop you from making this crisp. A little extra lemon zest will zip it up just fine.

1 cup [200 g] firmly packed light brown sugar

1½ cups [120 g] rolled oats

¼ cup [30 g] unbleached all-purpose flour, plus 3 Tbsp

6 Tbsp [85 g] unsalted butter, softened

½ tsp ground cinnamon

⅛ tsp kosher salt

4 nectarines, pitted and each cut into about 8 wedges

2 cups [240 g] fresh blueberries

1½ cups [180 g] fresh blackberries

1½ cups [180 g] fresh raspberries

2 Tbsp chopped lemon verbena

Zest and juice of ½ lemon

Frozen Lemon Kefir (page 109) or whipped cream for serving (optional)

Preheat the oven to 400°F [200°C]. Grease a 2-qt [2-L] baking pan.

Combine ½ cup [100 g] of the brown sugar, the oats, ¼ cup [30 g] flour, butter, cinnamon, and salt in a medium bowl. Mix together with your fingers or a fork until well blended. Set aside.

Combine the nectarines, blueberries, blackberries, and raspberries in a large bowl. Add the remaining ½ cup [100 g] brown sugar (less if your fruit is at its peak of ripeness), the 3 Tbsp flour, lemon verbena, lemon zest, and lemon juice and toss gently to combine. Transfer to the prepared baking pan and sprinkle the oat mixture evenly over the fruit.

Bake for about 40 minutes, or until the fruit is bubbly and the topping is crisp. Let cool on a wire rack for 15 minutes, then serve warm with frozen lemon kefir, if desired. Store, covered, at room temperature for up to 24 hours.

SERVES 8

LEMONY STRAWBERRY-RHUBARB COBBLER

12 oz [340 g] rhubarb, stalks halved lengthwise and diced

3 cups [360 g] strawberries, sliced

1 cup [200 g] granulated sugar, plus 3 Tbsp

½ cup [100 g] firmly packed light brown sugar

4 Tbsp cornstarch

½ tsp kosher salt

Zest of 2 lemons, plus 1 Tbsp fresh lemon juice

2 cups [240 g] unbleached all-purpose flour

1 Tbsp baking powder

½ cup [110 g] cold unsalted butter, cubed

¾ cup [180 ml] buttermilk

1 large egg

2 Tbsp turbinado or granulated sugar (optional)

Whipped cream or vanilla ice cream for serving

Start to finish: 1 hour
Hands-on time: 30 minutes

My mother-in-law, Mary Snyder, makes the most memorable rhubarb pie I've ever eaten. Since I can't compete with her most excellent pie, I have set my sights on making rhubarb cobbler. It's a little easier and less time consuming to prepare, and if you've never tasted Mary's rhubarb pie, you might think this cobbler is the best rhubarb dessert in the world.

Preheat the oven to 400°F [200°C]. Grease a 2-qt [2-L] baking pan.

Combine the rhubarb, strawberries, 1 cup [200 g] granulated sugar, brown sugar, cornstarch, ¼ tsp of the salt, half of the lemon zest, and the lemon juice in a large bowl and toss together. Set aside.

Combine the flour, baking powder, butter, 3 Tbsp granulated sugar, remaining ¼ tsp salt, and remaining zest in a medium bowl. Rub the mixture together with your thumb and forefinger in a snapping motion until the butter is blended together and no large lumps remain. Beat the buttermilk and egg with a fork in a small bowl. Pour it evenly over the flour mixture and mix with the fork until the dough just comes together. It should resemble loose biscuit dough.

continued

pastries,
43 cobblers,
tarts, and
pies

Heap the fruit into the prepared baking pan. Scatter the dough evenly over the top, breaking it up with your fingers to make equal-size chunks. Sprinkle with the turbinado sugar (if using; it adds a bit of crunch).

Bake for about 35 minutes, or until the top is browned and the filling is bubbly. Let cool slightly and serve warm with whipped cream. The cobbler can be baked in the morning on the day it will be served and kept at room temperature for up to 8 hours, or covered, in the refrigerator for up to 2 days. If you'd like to serve it warm, reheat in a 350°F [180°C] oven for about 10 minutes.

SERVES 8

pastries,
45 cobblers,
tarts, and
pies

ROASTED PEAR TART
WITH LIMONCELLO CUSTARD AND ROSEMARY—CORNMEAL CRUST

Start to finish:
2 hours, 30 minutes
Hands-on time: 40 minutes

Italians have a habit of using cornmeal in their desserts, so when I thought about adding some rosemary to pie dough, it seemed like a good idea to throw in a little texture via cornmeal as well. This rustic, rosemary-infused crust is perfect with roasted ripe pears and boozy limoncello custard. There are a few steps here, but they are all worth it.

ZESTY TIP

Roasting pears brings out their softer, sweeter side, but you'll get the most flavor from pears that have had a rest on your countertop for a few days. Look for them to change from bright green to yellowish green. That's when they taste best.

PASTRY

1¼ cups [150 g] unbleached all-purpose flour

⅓ cup [45 g] fine yellow cornmeal

1 Tbsp sugar

½ tsp kosher salt

2 tsp minced fresh rosemary

½ cup plus 2 Tbsp [135 g] cold unsalted butter, cubed

¼ cup plus 2 Tbsp [90 ml] ice water

4 Anjou or Bartlett pears, peeled, cored, and each cut into 6 wedges

2 Tbsp unsalted butter, melted

3 Tbsp sugar

Pinch of kosher salt

CUSTARD

½ cup [100 g] sugar

2 Tbsp cornstarch

2 large eggs

Pinch of kosher salt

½ cup [120 ml] heavy cream

Zest of 1 lemon

3 Tbsp limoncello

TO MAKE THE PASTRY: Combine the flour, cornmeal, sugar, salt, rosemary, and butter in a small bowl and place in the freezer for at least 30 minutes, or up to 1 hour.

Remove the flour mixture from the freezer and put in the bowl of a food processor. Pulse about ten times to cut the butter into the flour. Quickly pour the ice water through the feed tube while pulsing another ten times. The dough will still look shaggy and rough (to achieve a tender, flaky pastry, don't overprocess at this point). Turn the pastry out onto a work surface and compress into a disk with your hands. You may have to knead the dough lightly with the heel of your hand to bring it together. Wrap in plastic wrap and refrigerate for about 30 minutes (this will make it easier to roll out).

sweet
and tart

Position a rack in the lower third of the oven, and preheat the oven to 400°F [200°C]. Line a baking sheet with parchment paper.

Toss the pears with the melted butter, sugar, and salt. Spread them out on the prepared baking sheet and roast, stirring once or twice, for about 20 minutes, or until they are softened and browned around the edges. Let cool completely. Leave the oven on.

TO MAKE THE CUSTARD: Whisk the sugar, cornstarch, eggs, and salt in a medium bowl until combined. Gradually whisk in the cream, lemon zest, and limoncello.

Roll out the chilled dough on a lightly floured work surface into a 16-in [40.5-cm] round, fold it in half, and transfer to a 9-in [23-cm] tart pan with a removable bottom. Unfold the dough and gently push the sides down into the corners of the pan, leaving the overhanging pastry on the outside. Roll the rolling pin over the top of the pan to trim the excess pastry and discard it. Press the sides of the pastry so that it comes slightly above the edge of the pan.

Arrange the cooled pears evenly on top of the dough, adding any caramelized sugar from the pan. Slowly pour in the custard. Depending on the size of your pears, you may not be able to fit all of the custard in the pan; fill it to within about ¼ in [6 mm] of the rim. (Do not overfill to the point that the custard will spill as you transfer the pan to the oven.) Place the tart on a baking sheet.

Bake for about 35 minutes, or until the custard is puffy and set. Let cool completely on a wire rack. Remove the rim from the pan, cut the tart, and serve. This tart is best served the day it is made. Store leftovers, covered, in the refrigerator for up to 2 days. Bring to room temperature before serving.

SERVES 8

pastries,
47 cobblers,
tarts, and
pies

TRIPLE-CITRUS TART
WITH CHOCOLATE CRUST AND BERRIES

Start to finish: 3 hours
Hands-on time: 1 hour

A few years ago, cookbook author Melissa Clark had the bright idea to mix lemon, blood orange, and lime juice all together to make a citrus curd. I think it's time we revisited this idea.

"Bright" doesn't even begin to describe the flavor of this tart, and don't get me started on the lovely pale color—I could live in a room that hue. The chocolate crust is perfect and adds just the right heft of cocoa flavor to this light yet rich assemblage topped with bright red raspberries and luscious blackberries.

CHOCOLATE CRUST

42 chocolate wafers (I use Nabisco Famous Chocolate Wafers)

¼ cup [50 g] sugar

½ cup [110 g] unsalted butter, melted

CITRUS CURD

2 lemons

2 blood oranges

1 lime

¾ cup [150 g] sugar

6 Tbsp [85 g] unsalted butter

Pinch of kosher salt

3 large eggs, plus 3 egg yolks

GLAZE

¼ cup [85 g] strained apricot jam

1 Tbsp corn syrup

1½ cups [180 g] blackberries

1½ cups [180 g] raspberries

TO MAKE THE CHOCOLATE CRUST: Preheat the oven to 350°F [180°C]. Combine the chocolate wafers and sugar in the bowl of a food processor and process until finely ground. Pour in the melted butter and process until well mixed and crumbly.

Dump the crumbs into a 9-in [23-cm] springform pan and, using the bottom of a glass or measuring cup, press the crumbs on the bottom and 1 in [2.5 cm] up the sides of the pan. Bake for about 15 minutes, or until fragrant and firm. Let cool completely on a wire rack.

TO MAKE THE CITRUS CURD: Zest the lemons, blood oranges, and lime; set the zests aside. Squeeze the citrus juice (you should have about 1 cup [240 ml]) and combine it with the sugar, butter, and salt in a medium saucepan. Bring the mixture to a boil over medium heat, stirring occasionally.

continued

Meanwhile, whisk the eggs and egg yolks in a medium heat-proof bowl until combined. While whisking rapidly, pour the hot citrus-sugar mixture slowly into the eggs. Return the egg mixture to the saucepan and cook over medium heat, stirring constantly with a heat-proof spatula, until lightly thickened, 2 to 3 minutes (do not boil or the eggs will curdle). The curd should coat the back of the spatula. It will thicken further as it cools.

Immediately transfer the citrus curd to a clean heat-proof bowl (otherwise it will continue to cook in the hot pan and could scramble) and stir in the zests. Continue stirring for 1 minute to stop the cooking and then let continue to cool at room temperature for 30 minutes.

Pour the curd into the cooled shell. Refrigerate the tart, covered, for at least 2 hours, or up to 24 hours, to set up.

TO MAKE THE GLAZE: Combine the jam and corn syrup in a small saucepan over medium heat and heat, stirring, until thinned and warm, about 1 minute.

Garnish the top of the tart with a circle of blackberries around the edge and fill in with the raspberries. Brush the warm (not hot) glaze over the berries to give them shine. Refrigerate for up to 8 hours before serving. (It will still be good the next day, but the berries will begin to soften.)

SERVES 8

sweet and tart

MILE-HIGH LEMON MERINGUE PIE

½ recipe Flaky Pastry
(page 170), rolled and fitted
into a 9-in [23-cm] pie plate

2 cups [400 g] sugar

¼ cup [25 g] cornstarch

Pinch of kosher salt

4 large eggs, separated, at
room temperature

1¼ cups [300 ml] water, plus
⅓ cup [80 ml]

Zest of 2 lemons, plus ⅓ cup
[80 ml] fresh lemon juice

2 Tbsp unsalted butter

Start to finish:
1 hour, 30 minutes
Hands-on time: 1 hour

A longtime favorite of the diner set, lemon meringue pie is equally about the lemon *and* the meringue. This recipe utilizes Italian meringue, which is a cooked and more stable version than the ones typically used on lemon meringue pie. It never weeps (you know, those little beads of sugary liquid that can dot the surface), and the benefit of cooked egg whites over raw is obvious. This meringue has a marshmallowy texture that I find addictive.

Preheat the oven to 400°F [200°C].

Chill the pie shell in the refrigerator for 30 minutes. Line it with a piece of parchment paper with a 4-in [10-cm] over-hang and fill it with pie weights (or rice or dried beans). Bake for 20 minutes. Remove the weights and continue baking the shell for another 10 to 15 minutes, or until brown and crisp. Let cool completely on a wire rack.

Combine 1 cup [200 g] of the sugar, the cornstarch, and salt in a medium saucepan. Whisk in the egg yolks and 1¼ cups [300 ml] water. Cook over medium heat, whisk-ing, until the filling thickens, 5 to 6 minutes. It should be pretty thick, like a pudding. Remove the pan from the heat and stir in the lemon zest, lemon juice, and butter. Set aside and keep warm in the pan while you make the meringue.

Combine the remaining 1 cup [200 g] sugar and ⅓ cup [80 ml] water in a small saucepan over medium-high heat. Bring to a boil and cook until the sugar syrup registers 240°F [115°C] on a candy thermometer, about 5 minutes.

continued

pastries,
51 cobblers,
tarts, and
pies

(If you don't have a candy thermometer, cook until it thickens slightly and then drop a small amount into a bowl of cool water. When it forms a rubbery soft ball, it's done.)

In a mixer bowl, whip the egg whites on high speed to soft peaks, then carefully pour in the hot sugar syrup in a steady stream. Continue to beat until the whites are cool.

Position a rack in the upper third of the oven, and preheat the broiler.

Pour the filling into the cooled pie shell and smooth the top. Spoon the meringue over the filling and make fluffy peaks with the back of the spoon. Be sure to cover the filling completely and anchor the meringue all the way to the edges of the crust.

Broil the pie for 30 seconds, or until the peaks are browned. (Alternatively, use a kitchen torch to brown the meringue; this makes it look so much prettier.) Let the meringue cool for 5 minutes. Store, covered, in the refrigerator for up to 24 hours. (Chilling the pie will make the crust tough, but it will still taste good the next day.) Bring to room temperature before serving.

SERVES 8

LEMON CHIFFON PIE

Start to finish: 4 hours
Hands-on time: 1 hour

Lemon chiffon is lemon meringue's brother from another mother. They're very similar but also uniquely different. I love how the fluffy mousselike texture of this chiffon pie contrasts with the crispy, crunchy crust. That opposition makes it deliciously interesting.

ZESTY TIP

Cooking the egg yolks for this silky pie is really simple. It's all about the bowl and the pan size. You want the bowl to fit down into the pan 3 to 4 in [7.5 to 10 cm], but not allow the bottom to touch the water. Then maintain the water at a simmer, not a boil, and whisk constantly to keep the yolks moving. That will help them cook evenly, and you won't have hot spots that might cause the yolks to curdle. I use the stainless-steel bowl from my stand mixer. It works perfectly.

½ recipe Flaky Pastry (page 170), rolled and fitted into a 9-in [23-cm] pie plate

1½ tsp unflavored gelatin

⅓ cup [80 ml] cold water

4 large eggs, separated

⅔ cup [130 g] sugar

Zest of 1 lemon, plus ¼ cup [60 ml] fresh lemon juice,

½ cup [120 ml] cold whipping cream

Preheat the oven to 375°F [190°C].

Chill the pie shell in the refrigerator for 30 minutes. Line it with a piece of parchment paper with a 4-in [10-cm] overhang and fill it with pie weights (or rice or dried beans). Bake for 20 minutes. Remove the weights and continue baking the shell for another 10 to 15 minutes, or until brown and crisp. Let cool completely on a wire rack.

Bring a saucepan of water to a simmer.

Meanwhile, sprinkle the gelatin over the ⅓ cup [80 ml] cold water in a small bowl and let soften for 5 minutes.

Fill a large bowl with ice and water. Set the ice bath aside.

Whip the egg yolks and ⅓ cup [65 g] of the sugar in a mixer bowl on medium-high speed until fluffy, then beat in the lemon zest and lemon juice. Place the mixer bowl over the saucepan of simmering water and cook, whisking constantly, until the mixture is thickened and coats the back of a spoon, 7 to 8 minutes. Be careful not to let the bowl touch the water or the egg yolks may heat too quickly and scramble (see Zesty Tip).

Remove the bowl from the heat and whisk in the gelatin mixture until dissolved. Place the bowl in the ice bath and stir with a rubber spatula to cool the yolk mixture to room temperature. Remove it from the ice bath and let sit while you whip the egg whites. (Don't overchill at this point or the gelatin will start to set.)

Whip the egg whites in a clean mixer bowl on high speed until soft peaks form. Gradually sprinkle in the remaining ⅓ cup [65 g] sugar and whip until glossy and the sugar has dissolved.

Whip the cream in another bowl on high speed until soft peaks form.

Fold one-third of the egg white mixture into the lemon mixture with a rubber spatula, then fold in the remaining whites. Carefully fold in the whipped cream just until mixed (overfolding will deflate it). Pour the mousse into the cooled pie shell, smooth the top, and refrigerate for 2 hours to set the filling. Serve well chilled. Store, covered, in the refrigerator for up to 24 hours. (The pie will still taste good, but the crust won't be as crisp.)

SERVES 8

pastries,
55 cobblers,
tarts, and
pies

SHAKER LEMON PIE

Start to finish: 1 hour,
40 minutes, plus overnight
Hands-on time: 50 minutes

Shakers had a tendency to be thrifty, so it makes sense that they would use the entire lemon—not just the juice or the zest—in this dessert. If you really love lemon, this pie will satisfy like no other. It's also uber-rich, so I suggest cutting it into smaller slices than usual.

3 large lemons

1¾ cups [350 g] granulated sugar

¼ tsp kosher salt

3 large eggs, beaten

4 Tbsp [55 g] unsalted butter, melted

3 Tbsp unbleached all-purpose flour

2 Tbsp sour cream

1 recipe Flaky Pastry (page 170), half rolled and fitted into a 9-in [23-cm] pie plate, half rolled into a 16-in circle and refrigerated

2 Tbsp whole milk

Turbinado sugar for sprinkling (optional)

Wash and dry the lemons. Trim the pointy ends and slice two of the lemons as thinly as possible using a mandoline or a very sharp knife. The slices should drape over the knife if laid on top of it. Remove the seeds.

Zest the remaining lemon and set the zest aside. Peel the white pith off the lemon and slice the flesh thinly, removing the seeds. Toss all of the lemon slices and the lemon zest with the granulated sugar and salt in a large bowl. Cover with plastic wrap and let sit at room temperature for at least 8 hours, or up to 24 hours, to soften.

Position a rack in the lower third of the oven, and preheat the oven to 425°F [220°C].

Add the eggs, melted butter, flour, and sour cream to the bowl with the softened lemon slices, mixing well.

sweet
and tart

Turn the lemon filling into the pie shell and fit the remaining pastry on top. Trim the top edges evenly with the edge of the pan and flip the bottom pastry up and over the top pastry to seal. Press it together and make a decorative edge. Brush the top of the pie with the milk, and cut three or four slits on the top for steam to escape. Sprinkle with the turbinado sugar (if using).

Bake for 25 minutes. Lower the oven temperature to 350°F [180°C] and bake for another 25 minutes, or until the top is golden. Let cool on a wire rack to room temperature so the filling can firm up. Store, covered, in the refrigerator for up to 24 hours. (Chilling the pie will make the crust tough, but it will still taste good the next day.) Bring to room temperature before serving.

SERVES 10

pastries,
57 cobblers,
tarts, and
pies

GRAPEFRUIT CUSTARD PIE

Start to finish: 2 hours
Hands-on time: 30 minutes

I was intrigued with this recipe by Emily and Melissa Elsen of *The Four & Twenty Blackbirds Pie Book* fame, since I'd never encountered a grapefruit pie, not to mention a saltine crust. Both are fabulous, as it turns out. Thanks for the inspiration, ladies. I'll be making more saltine crusts in the future. This pie is awesome, but up the ante by garnishing with whipped cream and candied citrus.

35 unsalted saltine crackers

3 Tbsp sugar, plus 1 cup [200 g]

7 Tbsp [100 g] unsalted butter, melted

¼ cup [85 g] honey

2 Tbsp unbleached all-purpose flour

½ tsp kosher salt

3 large eggs, plus 1 egg yolk

1 cup [240 ml] fresh grapefruit juice

2 Tbsp Campari liqueur

¾ cup [180 ml] heavy cream

Dash of orange bitters (optional)

Position a rack in the lower third of the oven, and preheat the oven to 375°F [190°C].

Combine the saltines and 3 Tbsp sugar in the bowl of a food processor and process until finely ground. Pour in 5 Tbsp [70 g] of the melted butter and pulse until the crumbs are evenly moistened.

Dump the crumbs into a 9-in [23-cm] glass pie plate and, using the bottom of a glass or measuring cup, press the crumbs on the bottom and all the way up the sides. Chill in the freezer for about 10 minutes. Bake for about 20 minutes, or until lightly golden. Let cool completely on a wire rack. Turn the oven temperature to 325°F [165°C].

Whisk the 1 cup [200 g] sugar, honey, flour, salt, remaining 2 Tbsp melted butter, eggs, and egg yolk in a large bowl until combined. Whisk in the grapefruit juice, Campari, cream, and bitters (if using). Strain through a fine-mesh strainer into the cooled shell.

Bake for 50 minutes, or until set but still wiggly in the center. Let cool completely on a wire rack. Store, covered, in the refrigerator for up to 2 days. Bring to room temperature before serving.

SERVES 8

CHAPTER 3
CAKES

If a cake from scratch makes any occasion special, a cake with citrus flavors makes it a veritable event. And there's seemingly no end to the possible variations on the spectrum. Lemon syrup–soaked layers, towering blood orange cake, herb infused, berry filled, and fruit studded—there's a world of bright-flavored cakes inside this chapter just waiting to be discovered.

LEMON CAKE
WITH LEMON-MASCARPONE FROSTING

Start to finish: 9 hours
Hands-on time:
1 hour, 30 minutes

Every baker needs an impressive celebration cake in their repertoire, and this could be THE ONE. Four layers—count them—brushed with lemon syrup and layered with lemon curd and mascarpone cheese whipped cream. Are you game?

To make this an orange cake, substitute Orange Curd (page 159) for the lemon curd; for the cake, use orange zest instead of lemon and orange extract instead of lemon; and for the syrup, substitute orange juice for the lemon juice and Cointreau for the limoncello.

ZESTY TIP

The cakes can be baked up to 1 day in advance; store, wrapped in plastic wrap, at room temperature. The mascarpone frosting can be made up to 1 day ahead; store, covered, in the refrigerator.

CAKE

2⅔ cups [320 g] sifted cake flour

2 tsp baking powder

½ tsp kosher salt

¾ cup [170 g] unsalted butter, softened

1¼ cups [250 g] granulated sugar

Zest of 1 lemon

2 large eggs, plus 2 egg yolks, at room temperature

2 tsp lemon extract

1 tsp vanilla extract

1 cup [240 ml] whole milk

LEMON SYRUP

½ cup [100 g] granulated sugar

½ cup [120 ml] water

⅓ cup [80 ml] fresh lemon juice

2 Tbsp limoncello

LEMON-MASCARPONE FROSTING

2 cups [480 ml] heavy cream, chilled

¾ cup [90 g] powdered sugar

1 lb [455 g] mascarpone cheese, softened

1 cup [280 g] Lemon Curd (page 158)

1 cup [280 g] Lemon Curd (page 158), chilled

TO MAKE THE CAKE: Preheat the oven to 350°F [180°C]. Grease two 9-in [23-cm] round cake pans. Line the bottoms with parchment paper, then grease and flour the parchment.

Whisk the flour, baking powder, and salt in a medium bowl until combined. Set aside.

Beat the butter, granulated sugar, and lemon zest in a mixer bowl on high speed until light and fluffy. Beat in the eggs and egg yolks, one at a time, then beat in the lemon extract and vanilla. Stop the mixer and scrape down the sides of the bowl. Turn the speed to low and add the flour mixture and milk in three additions, beginning with the

sweet
and tart

flour and ending with the milk, beating for 30 seconds after each addition. Scrape down the sides of the bowl as necessary.

Divide the batter between the prepared pans and smooth the tops. Bake for 20 to 25 minutes, or until a tester or wooden skewer inserted into the center comes out clean and the cakes spring back when gently pressed. Let cool in the pans on wire racks for 10 minutes, then turn the cakes out onto the racks. Peel off the parchment and let cool completely before frosting.

TO MAKE THE SYRUP: Combine the granulated sugar, water, and lemon juice in a small saucepan over medium heat and stir until the sugar is dissolved. Remove from the heat and let cool slightly, then stir in the limoncello. Set aside.

TO MAKE THE FROSTING: Whip the cream with the powdered sugar in a mixer bowl on high speed until soft peaks form. Turn the speed to medium-low and whip in the mascarpone cheese and lemon curd. Cover and refrigerate the frosting if not using right away.

Cut each cake in half horizontally using a long serrated knife (the layers may be thin). Carefully place one cake layer, cut-side up, on a serving plate. Working quickly so the frosting and lemon curd remain cold, brush the cake with about ¼ cup [60 ml] of the syrup and spread about one-third of the chilled lemon curd over the top. Spread about 1 cup [240 ml] of the frosting on top and place another cake layer, cut-side up, on top. Continue to layer syrup, lemon curd, frosting, and cake until the last layer is brushed with syrup. Spread the top and sides of the cake with frosting. Transfer the remaining frosting to a pastry bag fitted with a rosette tip. Pipe the frosting decoratively over the top of the cake.

Refrigerate for at least 6 hours, or up to 2 days, so the cake absorbs the flavors and moisture. Serve cold from the refrigerator (the frosting can melt a bit if it becomes warm).

SERVES 10 TO 12

LEMONY ROSE GERANIUM CAKE

Start to finish:
2 hours, plus cooling
Hands-on time: 30 minutes

I started making this cake back in the 1980s after working with two lovely Texan ladies, Gwen Barclay and her mother, the late Madalene Hill. I fell in love with this cake during their cooking class on how to use herbs, and have grown a rose geranium plant every summer since then just to make this lovely treat. One of its charms is the floral aroma, and the other is that it uses lemon-lime soda as the leavener, an old country trick employed when baking powder was scarce. This is delicious topped with Lemon Curd (page 158), Meyer Lemon Ice Cream (page 106), or fresh fruit.

6 rose geranium leaves, stemmed

1½ cups [330 g] unsalted butter, at room temperature

3 cups [600 g] sugar

Pinch of kosher salt

1 tsp orange extract

5 large eggs, at room temperature

3 cups [360 g] unbleached all-purpose flour

1 cup [240 ml] lemon-lime soda (full sugar, not diet), at room temperature

Zest of 2 lemons, plus ¼ cup [60 ml] fresh lemon juice

Preheat the oven to 325°F [165°C]. Line two 5-by-9-in [12-by-23-cm] loaf pans with parchment paper. Cut four strips of parchment. Place two in each pan to fit along the bottom and up the sides, with overhang at the top to help pull the loaves out of the pans. Grease the parchment. Line the pans with the geranium leaves, top-side down.

Beat the butter and sugar in a mixer bowl on medium speed until light and fluffy. Beat in the salt, orange extract, and then the eggs, one at a time. Stop the mixer and scrape down the sides of the bowl. Turn the speed to low and add the flour and soda in three additions, beginning with the flour and ending with the soda, then stir in the lemon zest and juice.

Pour the batter into the prepared pans and smooth the tops. Bake for 90 minutes, or until a wooden skewer inserted into the center comes out with dry crumbs attached. Let cool in the pans on a wire rack for 30 minutes, then lift the cakes from the pans using the parchment paper. Remove the paper and let cool completely. Store, wrapped in plastic wrap, at room temperature for up to 3 days.

MAKES 2 LOAVES

LEMONY PLUM UPSIDE-DOWN CAKE

1 cup [120 g] unbleached all-purpose flour

½ tsp baking powder

½ tsp baking soda

¼ tsp kosher salt

8 Tbsp [110 g] unsalted butter, softened

¾ cup [150 g] sugar

1 large egg

Zest of 1 lemon, plus 2 tsp fresh lemon juice

⅓ cup [80 ml] buttermilk

1 tsp vanilla extract

3 plums, pitted and each cut into 12 slices

Start to finish:
1 hour, 15 minutes
Hands-on time: 30 minutes

I always loved pineapple upside-down cake as a child, but now I find it's a little too sweet for my taste. However, this plum version featuring bright purple fruit punctuated with lemon is a stunner . . . just make it once and it will become a regular on your dessert short list.

Preheat the oven to 350°F [180°C].

Whisk the flour, baking powder, baking soda, and salt in a small bowl. Set aside.

Beat 6 Tbsp [85 g] of the butter and ½ cup [100 g] of the sugar in a mixer bowl on high speed until light and fluffy. Add the egg and lemon zest and beat until well blended and creamy. Turn the speed to low and add the flour mixture and buttermilk in three additions, beginning with the flour and ending with the buttermilk, beating until smooth. Beat in the vanilla. Set the batter aside.

Melt the remaining 2 Tbsp butter in a 9-in [23-cm] round cake pan over medium heat. Add the remaining ¼ cup [50 g] sugar and cook, stirring, for about 2 minutes. It doesn't need to be brown but should be bubbly. Carefully remove the pan from the heat and spread the melted sugar evenly over the bottom of the pan. Working from the center to the outside, arrange the plum slices in a decorative pattern, overlapping them slightly. Sprinkle with the lemon juice. Return the pan to medium heat and

continued

cook undisturbed for 4 minutes, or until the juices bubble up and around the plums. Turn down the heat if needed to keep the fruit from browning. Remove the pan from the heat.

Carefully and evenly spoon the batter over the fruit slices (try not to disturb their placement). Bake for 25 minutes, or until a wooden skewer inserted into the center comes out clean. Let cool in the pan on a wire rack for 10 minutes (no more, or it might stick), then invert the cake onto a serving plate. Store, covered, at room temperature for up to 24 hours.

SERVES 8

LEMONY CREAM CHEESE POUND CAKE

Start to finish: 3 hours
Hands-on time: 40 minutes

Does a pound cake *have* to include a whole pound of butter? How about swapping out some of the butter with cream cheese? The velvety, rich taste only makes pound cake extra-delicious, and I think the addition of citrusy zest and a tart lemony glaze is sure to brighten any day. Serve it to a crowd with sliced fresh fruit or sorbet; this hefty cake loves to soak up all that sweet fruit juice.

3 cups [360 g] sifted cake flour

1 tsp baking powder

½ tsp kosher salt

1½ cups [330 g] unsalted butter, softened

8 oz [230 g] cream cheese, softened

3⅓ cups [665 g] sugar

Zest of 4 lemons, plus ⅔ cup [160 ml] fresh lemon juice

6 large eggs, at room temperature

Preheat the oven to 350°F [180°C]. Grease and flour a 12-cup [2.8-L] or 10-in [25-cm] Bundt pan.

Sift the flour, baking powder, and salt into a small bowl. Set aside.

Beat the butter and cream cheese in a mixer bowl on medium speed until creamy. Add 3 cups [600 g] of the sugar and the lemon zest and beat until light and fluffy. Add ⅓ cup [80 ml] of the lemon juice and beat until blended. Turn the speed to low and add the eggs, one at a time, beating until well combined. Add the flour mixture in three additions, beating until smooth.

Pour the batter into the prepared pan and smooth the top. Set the pan on a baking sheet and turn the oven temperature to 325°F [165°C]. Bake for 60 to 75 minutes, or until a wooden skewer inserted into the center comes out clean. Let cool in the pan on a wire rack for 15 minutes, then unmold the cake and turn it right-side up.

Combine the remaining ⅓ cup [65 g] sugar and ⅓ cup
[80 ml] lemon juice in a small saucepan over medium
heat and stir just until the sugar is dissolved. Set the rack
with the cake over a baking sheet to catch the drips and
brush the glaze over the warm cake. Let cool completely.
Store, covered, at room temperature for up to 2 days.

SERVES 10 TO 12

LEMON-ALMOND CAKE
WITH BASIL-HONEYED BERRIES

Start to finish: 2 hours
Hands-on time: 15 minutes

Hello. Meet your new best friend . . . almond cake.

There are many reasons to love almond cake. First, unlike your favorite cashmere scarf, it's as deliciously adaptable in the heat of summer as in the throes of winter. Here, I've paired it up with basil-scented berries, but any juicy fruit would do. It gets along with all of your fruity friends.

ZESTY TIP

Look for almond paste in a can instead of packed in a plastic cylinder. Most pastry chefs find that canned paste is the best quality.

¾ cup [150 g] granulated sugar

8 oz [230 g] almond paste, broken into pieces

½ cup [110 g] unsalted butter, softened

Zest and juice of 1 lemon

1 tsp vanilla extract

3 large eggs, at room temperature

½ cup [60 g] unbleached all-purpose flour

1 tsp baking powder

¼ tsp kosher salt

2 cups [280 g] mixed sliced fresh strawberries and whole blackberries, blueberries, or raspberries

¼ cup [7 g] fresh basil leaves, rolled lengthwise into a tight cylinder and thinly sliced crosswise

2 Tbsp honey

Powdered sugar for dusting

Preheat the oven to 350°F [180°C]. Grease a 9-in [23-cm] round cake pan with 2-in [5-cm] sides. Line the bottom with parchment paper, then grease and flour the parchment.

Combine the granulated sugar and almond paste in the bowl of a food processor and pulse until finely blended. (Alternatively, beat in a stand mixer on medium speed until the almond paste has completely blended with the sugar.) Add the butter, lemon zest, and vanilla and pulse until smooth. Turn on the processor and add the eggs, one at a time, through the feed tube. Remove the lid and add the flour, baking powder, and salt. Cover and pulse a few more times just until blended. (If using a mixer, add the butter, lemon zest, and vanilla and beat on medium speed until evenly blended, then add the eggs, one at a time, and beat until smooth. Turn the speed to low, add the flour, baking powder, and salt, and beat until completely mixed.)

continued

Scrape the batter into the prepared pan and smooth the top. Bake for 45 to 50 minutes, or until the cake is golden and a wooden skewer inserted into the center comes out clean. Let cool in the pan on a wire rack for about 30 minutes, then loosen the sides with a knife if necessary, invert the cake onto a serving plate, and peel off the parchment.

Meanwhile, combine the berries, basil, honey, and lemon juice in a bowl and refrigerate for 30 minutes, or until juicy.

Slice the cooled cake with a serrated knife, and serve topped with the berries and a dusting of powdered sugar. Store, covered, at room temperature for up to 1 day.

SERVES 6 TO 8

sweet and tart

LEMON POLENTA CAKE

1¼ cups [150 g] unbleached all-purpose flour

¾ cup [105 g] fine yellow cornmeal

½ tsp kosher salt

¼ tsp baking powder

1 cup [200 g] sugar

¾ cup [170 g] unsalted butter, softened

Zest of 2 lemons, plus ¼ cup [60 ml] fresh lemon juice

4 large eggs, at room temperature

½ cup [120 ml] plain whole-milk Greek yogurt

Preheat the oven to 350°F [180°C]. Grease a 5-by-9-in [12-by-23-cm] loaf pan. Line it with parchment paper, leaving a bit of overhang, and grease the parchment.

Whisk the flour, cornmeal, salt, and baking powder in a small bowl until combined. Set aside.

Beat the sugar, butter, and lemon zest in a mixer bowl on high speed until fluffy. Add the eggs, one at a time, beating well after each addition and stopping the mixer to scrape down the sides of the bowl. Turn the speed to medium and beat in the yogurt and lemon juice. Turn the speed to low and add the flour mixture in three additions, then beat for another 1 minute, or until the batter is thick and creamy.

Pour the batter into the prepared pan and smooth the top. Bake for 50 to 55 minutes, or until a wooden skewer inserted into the center comes out clean. Let cool in the pan on a wire rack for 15 minutes, then lift the cake from the pan using the parchment paper. Remove the paper and let cool completely. Store, covered, at room temperature for up to 3 days, or freeze for up to 2 months.

SERVES 8

Start to finish:
2 hours, 30 minutes
Hands-on time: 30 minutes

"Polenta" is just another name for "cornmeal," but it gives this simple cake *sprezzatura*, an Italian term for "a studied carelessness." This unassuming cake is elegant when toasted and served with fresh fruit or ice cream. It says, "I know I'm a simple cornmeal cake, but I'm a fabulous cornmeal cake." For an interesting variation, slice the cake and toast the slices, serving them warm with fruit or Frozen Lemon Kefir (page 109).

BLOOD ORANGE ANGEL FOOD CAKE

Start to finish:
1 hour, 10 minutes
Hands-on time: 30 minutes

If there is a heaven, the angels make this cake there and serve it to you as you walk through the gates. Fluffy and light, the cake is the perfect ending to a meal when combined with fresh berries, orange slices, whipped cream, ice cream, or a fruity sorbet.

ZESTY TIPS

Because cake flour is lumpy, it must be sifted before measuring to ensure you are adding the correct amount. Just sift the flour onto a sheet of parchment paper and then spoon it into the measuring cup. Sift even if you are weighing the ingredients, as the flour will blend more evenly when sifted.

I call for a precise amount of egg whites in this recipe because the beaten whites are the leavening, or the reason that the cake is light and fluffy. If I measured by the number of eggs, and the whites were smaller than normal, there might not be enough whites to lift and give it the fluffiness expected in an angel food cake.

1¼ cups [150 g] sifted cake flour

1½ cups [300 g] superfine sugar

1½ cups [360 ml] egg whites, at room temperature

1 tsp vanilla extract

1 tsp cream of tartar

Kosher salt

Zest of 2 blood oranges or navel oranges, plus 3 Tbsp fresh orange juice

2 cups [200 g] powdered sugar, sifted

1 Tbsp orange-flavored liqueur, such as Cointreau

Preheat the oven to 375°F [190°C].

Dump the flour and ½ cup [100 g] of the superfine sugar into a sifter or a wire-mesh strainer set over a bowl.

Whip the egg whites, vanilla, cream of tartar, ½ tsp salt, and the orange zest in a mixer bowl on high speed just until soft peaks form. Slowly sprinkle in the remaining 1 cup [200 g] superfine sugar until stiff, glossy peaks form, stopping the mixer and scraping down the sides of the bowl once or twice.

If using a stand mixer, remove the bowl from the mixer. Sift the flour mixture into the whites in three additions, folding gently with a large spatula just until blended (no need to fold the flour in completely until the third addition). Be careful not to overfold or the egg whites will deflate.

continued

Pour the batter into a 10-by-4-in [25-by-10-cm] ungreased tube pan, preferably with a removable bottom, and smooth the top. Bake for about 40 minutes, or until the cake is golden and a tester or wooden skewer inserted into the cake comes out clean.

Remove the cake from the oven and immediately invert it onto the neck of a bottle or, if your pan has feet attached to it, invert it over a wire rack. Let cool completely, upside down.

Turn the cake right-side up and run a sharp knife around the outer edge of the pan and then around the center tube. Invert to release the cake, remove the pan, and run a sharp knife between the bottom of the cake and pan bottom to release. Transfer to a serving plate.

Combine the powdered sugar, orange juice, liqueur, and a pinch of salt in a medium bowl and blend with a fork to make a glaze. (Add more orange juice if the glaze is too thick; add more sugar if it is too thin.) Spoon the glaze over the top of the cake and let it drip down the sides. Store, covered, at room temperature for up to 3 days.

SERVES 8

sweet and tart

LIMONCELLO SHORTCAKES
WITH BERRIES AND MEYER LEMON ICE CREAM

2 cups [240 g] unbleached all-purpose flour

⅔ cup [130 g] granulated sugar

1 Tbsp baking powder

½ tsp kosher salt

½ cup [110 g] cold unsalted butter, cubed

Zest of 1 lemon

½ cup [120 ml] whipping cream, plus more for brushing

¼ cup [60 ml] limoncello, plus more for drizzling (chilled for at least 4 hours)

2 Tbsp turbinado or granulated sugar

3½ cups [500 g] fresh blackberries or blueberries

12 oz [340 g] fresh strawberries, sliced

Meyer Lemon Ice Cream (page 106) for serving

Meyer Lemon Ice Cream (page 106) for serving

Start to finish:
1 hour, 20 minutes
Hands-on time: 40 minutes

Since just about everything tastes better with limoncello, I decided to use it two ways in this recipe—as an ingredient in the shortcakes and as a delectable drizzle on top of the berries. Grandma's shortcakes were good, but these light and airy rounds are sure to delight the grown-up kid in you.

ZESTY TIP

Bake the shortcakes up to 4 hours in advance and store, covered, at room temperature.

Preheat the oven to 350°F [180°C]. Line a baking sheet with parchment paper.

Whisk the flour, ⅓ cup [65 g] of the granulated sugar, the baking powder, and salt in a large bowl. Add the butter and lemon zest and crumble the butter into the flour with your fingers. Add the cream and limoncello and stir with a fork just until a dough is formed.

Turn the dough out onto a lightly floured work surface and pat or roll it 1 in [2.5 cm] thick. Cut out rounds with a 3-in [7.5-cm] cutter and place on the prepared baking sheet. Gather up the scraps and repeat for a total of six rounds. Brush the tops with cream and sprinkle with the turbinado sugar. Bake for about 25 minutes, or until golden. Let cool on a wire rack.

Meanwhile, combine all the berries and the remaining ⅓ cup [65 g] granulated sugar in a bowl and toss to blend. Cover and refrigerate for up to 4 hours.

Split the shortcakes and place a scoop of ice cream and a few spoonfuls of the berries on the bottom rounds. Drizzle with limoncello and cover with the top rounds to serve.

SERVES 6

LEMON-FILLED COCONUT CUPCAKES

Start to finish: 2 hours
Hands-on time: 1 hour

Filled cupcakes beguile with hidden yummy centers. If you grew up loving those chocolate cupcakes with the squiggle on top, you're going to adore these coconutty, lemon-filled charmers. Made with coconut milk and topped with toasted coconut, these lemon curd–filled tiny cakes are a lot of fun, but go ahead and sub in Orange Curd (page 159) for the lemon if you're feeling adventurous.

2 cups [240 g] sifted cake flour

1½ tsp baking powder

¼ tsp baking soda

¼ tsp kosher salt

1 cup [220 g] unsalted butter, softened

1 cup [200 g] granulated sugar

1 tsp coconut extract

1 tsp vanilla extract

4 large eggs, at room temperature

¾ cup [180 ml] canned unsweetened coconut milk, stirred well

1½ cups [140 g] sweetened shredded coconut

3 cups [360 g] powdered sugar

2 Tbsp whole milk

1⅓ cups [375 g] Lemon Curd (page 158)

Preheat the oven to 350°F [180°C]. Line a 12-cup muffin pan with paper cups.

Whisk the flour, baking powder, baking soda, and salt in a small bowl until combined. Set aside.

Beat ½ cup [110 g] of the butter and the granulated sugar in a mixer bowl on high speed until light and fluffy. Add the coconut extract, ½ tsp of the vanilla, and then the eggs, one at a time. Stop the mixer and scrape down the sides of the bowl. Turn the speed to low and add the flour mixture in three additions, alternating with the coconut milk and beginning and ending with the flour, then beat on medium speed until smooth, about 1 minute.

Divide the batter among the prepared muffin cups (I like to use a ¼-cup [60-ml] ice-cream scoop), filling them almost to the top. Bake for 15 to 20 minutes, then rotate the pans 180 degrees and bake for another 5 minutes, until the tops spring back when lightly pressed. They will be pale. Let cool in the pan on a wire rack for 5 minutes, then transfer the cupcakes to the rack to cool completely. Leave the oven on.

sweet and tart

Spread the shredded coconut on a baking sheet and bake for 5 minutes. Stir the coconut and bake for another 2 to 3 minutes, or until golden and toasted. Remove from the oven and let cool. Transfer the coconut to a shallow bowl and set aside.

Beat the powdered sugar, milk, remaining ½ cup [110 g] butter, and remaining ½ tsp vanilla in a mixer bowl on medium speed until fluffy and light. (Add more milk if the frosting is too thick or more powdered sugar if it is too thin.) Set aside.

Remove a cone-shaped section from the top and center of each cupcake by using a cupcake corer (available at cook-ware shops) or by cutting a 1-in [2.5-cm] circle in the top of the cupcake and scooping out a cone-shaped section; save the pieces that you remove. (I like lots of filling, so I scoop a little more from the inside using a baby or demi-tasse spoon.) Using a pastry bag fitted with a large round tip, or a plastic bag with a hole cut in one of the corners, fill the cupcakes with lemon curd. Cut the bottoms from the reserved cone-shaped sections and fit the top back into each cupcake (go ahead and snack on the remnants).

Frost the cupcakes generously, and immediately dip the tops into the cooled coconut, pressing gently to help it adhere. Store, covered, in the refrigerator for up to 1 day. Bring to room temperature before serving.

MAKES 12 CUPCAKES

79
cakes

LEMON-BLACKBERRY CUPCAKES

Start to finish:
1 hour, 30 minutes
Hands-on time: 45 minutes

Though I usually find cupcakes on the twee side, these are special. I'm not sure if it's the ultra-lemony pound cake on the bottom or the tart, berry-hued buttercream. But then it could also be the big, fresh blackberry planted on top. If you want to make cupcakes with a wow factor, this is your recipe.

CUPCAKES

3 cups [360 g] unbleached all-purpose flour

1 tsp kosher salt

½ tsp baking powder

½ tsp baking soda

1 cup [220 g] unsalted butter, softened

2 cups [400 g] granulated sugar

5 large eggs

¾ cup [180 ml] sour cream

Zest of 2 lemons, plus ⅔ cup [160 ml] fresh lemon juice

BUTTERCREAM

1½ cups [220 g] blackberries

1 Tbsp granulated sugar

2 Tbsp fresh lemon juice

1 cup [220 g] unsalted butter, softened

5 cups [500 g] powdered sugar

¼ tsp kosher salt

Whole milk or half-and-half, if needed

24 blackberries

TO MAKE THE CUPCAKES: Preheat the oven to 350°F [180°C]. Line two 12-cup muffin pans with paper cups.

Whisk the flour, salt, baking powder, and baking soda in a medium bowl until combined. Set aside.

Beat the butter and granulated sugar in a mixer bowl on high speed until fluffy. Turn the speed to medium and add the eggs, one at a time, then the sour cream and lemon zest and beat until creamy. Turn the speed to low and add the flour mixture in three additions, alternating with the lemon juice and beginning and ending with the flour, beating until smooth and no lumps remain.

Divide the batter among the prepared muffin cups. Bake for 20 minutes, then rotate the pans 180 degrees and bake for another 5 minutes, or until the edges are golden and the cupcakes spring back when lightly pressed. Let cool completely in the pans on wire racks.

continued

TO MAKE THE BUTTERCREAM: Combine the blackberries, granulated sugar, and lemon juice in a small saucepan over medium heat, smashing the berries to a purée. Bring to a boil and let bubble for 1 minute. Remove from the heat and strain the mixture through a fine-mesh strainer. Discard the pulp. Let cool completely before continuing.

Beat the butter and 3 cups [300 g] of the powdered sugar in a mixer bowl on medium speed. Add the salt and 3 Tbsp of the berry purée, turn the speed to low, and slowly add the remaining 2 cups [200 g] powdered sugar. If the buttercream is too thick, thin it with a little milk. (You will have some berry purée left over; add to sparkling water for a fruity spritzer while you decorate the cupcakes.)

Fill a pastry bag fitted with a fluted or star tip and pipe the buttercream completely around the tops of the cupcakes. Nestle a fresh blackberry on top of each. Store in the refrigerator for up to 2 days (once the frosting has set up, cover the cupcakes). Bring to room temperature before serving.

MAKES 24 CUPCAKES

CARA CARA CHEESECAKE
WITH CHOCOLATE CRUST

42 chocolate wafers (I use Nabisco Famous Chocolate Wafers)

1¾ cups [350 g] sugar

6 Tbsp [85 g] unsalted butter, melted

1½ lb [680 g] cream cheese, softened

½ cup [120 ml] heavy cream

Zest of 3 Cara Cara oranges, plus ½ cup [120 ml] fresh Cara Cara orange juice

¼ cup [60 ml] Cointreau or other orange-flavored liqueur

1 tsp orange extract

½ tsp kosher salt

4 large eggs

Start to finish: 14 hours
Hands-on time: 30 minutes

Cara Cara oranges are my new citrus fetish. Seedless and with a pinkish-red flesh, Cara Caras have a tangy cranberry-like zing but with lower acid than most navel oranges. I love the bright orange flavor in this cheesecake juxtaposed with the black, chocolaty crust.

Preheat the oven to 350°F [180°C].

Combine the chocolate wafers and ¼ cup [50 g] of the sugar in the bowl of a food processor and process until finely ground. Pour in the melted butter and process until well mixed and evenly moistened.

Dump the crumbs into a 9-in [23-cm] springform pan and, using the bottom of a glass or measuring cup, press the crumbs on the bottom and 2 in [5 cm] up the sides of the pan. Bake for about 10 minutes, or until fragrant and firm. Let cool completely on a wire rack.

Beat the cream cheese and remaining 1½ cups [300 g] sugar in a mixer bowl on medium-high speed until light and fluffy, about 4 minutes, scraping down the sides of the bowl as necessary. Turn the speed to low; add the cream, orange zest, orange juice, Cointreau, orange extract, and salt; and beat until well mixed. Add the eggs, one at a time, beating just until combined and scraping down the sides of the bowl after each addition.

ZESTY TIP

As the cake cools, the crusty sides of this cheesecake contract. Loosening the sides of the pan from the crust will result in a prettier cheesecake with less cracking. Also, cooling the cake in the water bath helps it to cool more slowly, minimizing cracking as well.

continued

83
cakes

Bring about 3 qt [2.8 L] water to a boil in a large saucepan. Line the outside of the springform pan with a large sheet of heavy-duty aluminum foil that reaches the top of the pan. Set the springform pan inside a roasting pan and pour the filling into the cooled crust.

Pour the boiling water into a heat-proof pitcher. Pull the middle rack halfway out of the oven and set the roasting pan on the rack. Carefully pour the hot water into the roasting pan until it reaches halfway up the sides of the springform pan. Bake for 90 minutes or until the cheesecake puffs around the edges and the center moves just slightly when jiggled.

Remove the pan from the oven. Run a small, sharp knife around the pan sides to loosen the cheesecake and let cool in the water-filled roasting pan on a wire rack for 45 minutes. Transfer the springform pan to the rack and let cool to room temperature, another 2 hours. Cover tightly with plastic wrap (don't let the plastic touch the top of the cheesecake) and refrigerate for at least overnight, or up to 4 days. Serve chilled.

For the neatest slices when serving, cut the cheesecake with a knife dipped in hot water and wiped clean with a paper towel after each slice.

SERVES 10

CHAPTER 4

CHILLED AND FROZEN DESSERTS

Chilled citrus desserts hold a special sway over me. Cool and refreshing with a balance of tart and creamy, the desserts in this chapter feature the flavors and textures of oranges and lemons at their best.

LIMONCELLO LEMON MOUSSE
WITH BERRIES

Start to finish: 4 hours
Hands-on time: 45 minutes

Lemon mousse is one of those airy, mid-century-modern desserts that has never gone out of style. I remember my mom serving it at her monthly card club, along with those little buttery pastel mints and bridge mix. There were always a few "mouse" left over for the kids to nibble on.

This version is admittedly a little more sophisticated than Mom's, with a boozy kick from the limoncello and a fresh berry garnish. Sorry, kids, this one is for adults only.

ZESTY TIP

Rubbing the lemon with sugar cubes effectively captures the fruit's oil, transferring loads of lemon flavor without the little flakes of zest. For best results, choose thick-skinned lemons with a nubby surface, which contain more of this essential oil.

2½ tsp unflavored gelatin

⅓ cup [80 ml] limoncello

6 sugar cubes

2 lemons, plus ⅔ cup [160 ml] fresh lemon juice

3 large eggs, separated, at room temperature

¼ cup [50 g] granulated sugar, plus ⅓ cup [65 g]

Pinch of kosher salt

1 tsp lemon oil

¾ cup [180 ml] whipping cream, chilled, plus ½ cup [120 ml]

2 Tbsp powdered sugar

1½ cups [210 g] fresh raspberries, blueberries, or blackberries

Sprinkle the gelatin over the limoncello in a heat-proof measuring cup and let soften for 5 minutes.

Rub the edges of the sugar cubes over the lemons so they pick up the lemons' zest and oils. (Some lemons give up their zest more easily than others. Don't worry if the sugar cubes dissolve a little bit. They should turn bright yellow.) Drop the lemony cubes into the limoncello mixture.

Place the softened gelatin in a microwave and heat for 20 seconds to dissolve the gelatin and sugar. Alternatively, place the cup in a small saucepan of simmering water and stir until the graininess has dissolved. Set aside.

Whip the egg whites in a mixer bowl on high speed until frothy and soft peaks form. Sprinkle the ¼ cup [50 g] granulated sugar over the whites and beat until firm but not curdled, about 2 minutes. (It's better to underbeat the whites slightly than to overbeat them.) The whites should form a stiff peak when the beaters are lifted from the bowl. (If using a stand mixer, transfer the whites to another large bowl and continue with the recipe. There's no need to wash the bowl.)

sweet and tart

Beat the egg yolks, salt, and ⅓ cup [65 g] granulated sugar in the mixer bowl on medium speed for about 1 minute, or until light in color. Turn the speed to medium-high and beat until thick and pale yellow, about 4 minutes. Mix in the dissolved gelatin, lemon juice, and lemon oil until blended. Gently fold the lemon mixture into the beaten whites with a large spatula. Be careful not to overmix, as you will be folding in the whipped cream as well. (There's no need to wash the bowl.)

Beat the ¾ cup [180 ml] cream in the mixer bowl on high speed until firm enough to hold its shape. Fold the whipped cream completely into the lemon mousse mixture.

Spoon the mousse into individual dessert dishes, cups, or a large serving bowl. Cover and refrigerate for at least 3 hours, or up to 1 day.

When ready to serve, beat the ½ cup [120 ml] cream and powdered sugar in a mixer bowl on high speed until fluffy. Spoon the whipped cream on top of the mousse and garnish with the berries to serve.

SERVES 6

POTS DE CRÈME
WITH LEMONGRASS

Start to finish: 6 hours
Hands-on time: 30 minutes

Lemongrass isn't tart, but it lends a lovely citrusy aroma to these little French puddings. Kind of like a crème brûlée without the crispy topping, these custards are enhanced by a smidge of limoncello. Feel free to offer a tiny chilled shot on the side.

1 cup [240 ml] water

Zest of 1 lemon removed with a vegetable peeler (yellow part only), plus 1 Tbsp fresh lemon juice

4 stalks lemongrass, white part only, thinly sliced

⅔ cup [130 g] sugar

1 cup [240 ml] whipping cream

1 cup [240 ml] whole milk

7 egg yolks

Pinch of kosher salt

2 Tbsp limoncello

½ tsp vanilla extract

Combine the water, lemon zest, and lemongrass in a medium saucepan over medium-high heat and bring to a boil. Boil for about 6 minutes, or until reduced by half. Add the sugar and continue to boil, stirring to dissolve the sugar, for another 4 minutes, or until reduced by half again. Remove from the heat. Stir in the cream and milk.

Whisk the egg yolks and salt in a large bowl until combined, then gradually whisk in the hot cream mixture. Stir in the lemon juice, limoncello, and vanilla. Cover and let stand for 30 minutes to allow the flavors to develop.

Preheat the oven to 325°F [165°C]. Bring a medium saucepan of water to a boil. Set a strainer over a large measuring cup with a pouring spout. Place a kitchen towel in a 9-by-13-in [23-by-33-cm] baking pan and arrange six ½-cup [120-ml] ramekins in the bottom of the pan (the towel will keep the ramekins from sliding around). Place the pan on a baking sheet for easier transport. Trim a piece of aluminum foil to fit over the top.

Strain the custard through the strainer into the measuring cup and divide among the prepared ramekins.

Pour the boiling water into a heat-proof pitcher. Pull the middle rack halfway out of the oven and set the roasting pan on the rack. Carefully pour the hot water into the roasting pan (you may want to remove one of the ramekins to make this easier) until it reaches halfway up the sides of the ramekins. Seal the top of the pan with the foil. Bake for about 40 minutes, or until the custards are set but still jiggly in the middle.

Remove the ramekins from the oven, uncover, and let cool completely in the water-filled roasting pan. Cover the cooled custards and refrigerate for at least 4 hours, or up to 2 days. Serve cold.

SERVES 6

GOAT CHEESE CRÈME BRÛLÉE
WITH LEMON AND CARDAMOM

Start to finish: 6 hours
Hands-on time: 30 minutes

Every now and then even a classic can benefit from a little twist. So for this updated version of crème brûlée, I added bright lemon, a bit of aromatic cardamom, and a healthy dose of tangy goat cheese to the custard base.

ZESTY TIP

What is the best part of crème brûlée? For many, it's the crackly caramelized sugar topping. To make the best crunchy top, buy a propane torch at your local hardware store. It has more oomph than the little torches sold at cookware shops; plus it's less expensive, and you can use it to brown other things like the tops of casseroles, gratins, and even a roast chicken that looks a little anemic on the sides.

1½ cups [360 ml] heavy cream, chilled

1 cup [240 ml] half-and-half

¾ cup [150 g] turbinado or demerara sugar

Pinch of kosher salt

1 vanilla bean, halved lengthwise, or 2 tsp vanilla extract

2 tsp cardamom seeds, coarsely ground in a mortar and pestle until fragrant

Zest and juice of 1 lemon

3 oz [85 g] goat cheese, softened

5 egg yolks

Combine the cream, half-and-half, ½ cup [100 g] of the sugar, the salt, vanilla bean, cardamom, and lemon juice in a medium saucepan over medium heat and heat until the mixture steams. With a slotted spoon, transfer the vanilla bean halves to a cutting board. Using the flat side of a knife, run the blade down the length of the bean to remove the seeds. Add the seeds and vanilla pod to the hot cream mixture and bring to a simmer. Remove the pan from the heat, cover, and let sit for 15 minutes to allow the flavors to develop. Add the goat cheese and whisk to combine.

Preheat the oven to 300°F [150°C]. Bring a medium saucepan of water to a boil. Set a fine-mesh strainer over a large measuring cup with a pouring spout. Place a kitchen towel in a 9-by-13-in [23-by-33-cm] baking pan and arrange six ½-cup [120-ml] ramekins in the bottom of the pan (the towel will keep the ramekins from sliding around). Place the pan on a baking sheet for easier transport.

Whisk the egg yolks in a large bowl until combined. Pour about 1 cup [240 ml] of the cream mixture into the eggs, whisking vigorously. Add the remaining cream mixture in

sweet
and tart

a stream, whisking constantly. Strain the custard through the strainer into the measuring cup and divide among the prepared ramekins.

Pour the boiling water into a heat-proof pitcher. Pull the middle rack halfway out of the oven and set the roasting pan on the rack. Carefully pour the hot water into the roasting pan (you may want to remove one of the ramekins to make this easier) until it reaches halfway up the sides of the ramekins. Bake for about 40 minutes, or until the custards are set. They will still look jiggly, but not liquid and loose.

Remove the ramekins from the water and let cool on a wire rack. When the ramekins are cool enough to handle, transfer to a baking sheet, cover with plastic wrap, and refrigerate until very cold, at least 4 hours or up to 2 days.

About 1 hour before serving, combine the lemon zest and remaining ¼ cup [50 g] sugar in a small bowl. Sprinkle the tops of the custards with 2 to 3 tsp of the lemon sugar and flame (*brûlée*) the tops with a propane torch until the sugar caramelizes. If you don't have a torch, you can run them under the broiler until the sugar browns (this really heats up the custards, so avoid it if you can). Whichever method you use, return the custards to the refrigerator for 45 minutes to re-chill, as they are best served really cold. Flame the tops of the custards no more than 2 hours before serving or the caramel will soften and won't have that trademark hard crack to it.

SERVES 6

BLOOD ORANGE PANNA COTTA
WITH BLOOD ORANGE COMPOTE

Start to finish: 5 hours
Hands-on time: 45 minutes

To paraphrase food writer Russ Parsons, "The best panna cotta is like a dream of cream held together by faith and just a little bit of gelatin." I couldn't agree more except to say that the best panna cotta just might be this citrusy version garnished with a vanilla-spiked blood orange compote.

PANNA COTTA

½ cup [120 ml] fresh blood orange juice, plus zest of 2 blood oranges

1 Tbsp fresh lemon juice

2½ tsp unflavored gelatin

1 cup [240 ml] whipping cream

½ cup [100 g] sugar

1 vanilla bean, split lengthwise

Pinch of kosher salt

1½ cups [360 ml] buttermilk

BLOOD ORANGE COMPOTE

¼ cup [60 ml] water

¼ cup [50 g] sugar

2 Tbsp fresh lemon juice

1 vanilla bean, split lengthwise

Zest of 1 blood orange, plus 3 blood oranges, peeled and sectioned

TO MAKE THE PANNA COTTA: Lightly oil six 1-cup [240-ml] ramekins.

Combine the blood orange juice and lemon juice in a small bowl. Sprinkle the gelatin over the top and let soften for 5 minutes.

Combine the cream, sugar, vanilla bean, salt, and blood orange zest in a small saucepan over medium heat and bring to a simmer. Remove from the heat, pour in the gelatin mixture, and stir until the gelatin has dissolved. Cover and let steep for 30 minutes to blend the flavors. With a slotted spoon, transfer the vanilla bean halves to a cutting board. Using the flat side of a knife, run the blade down the length of the bean to remove the seeds. Add the seeds to the cream. Discard the pod (or rinse and dry it and reserve for another use).

continued

Pour the buttermilk into a large measuring cup with a pouring spout. Strain the cream mixture through a fine-mesh strainer into the buttermilk and stir to combine. Divide the panna cotta among the prepared ramekins, cover, and refrigerate until set, about 4 hours.

TO MAKE THE COMPOTE: Combine the water, sugar, lemon juice, vanilla bean, and blood orange zest in a small saucepan over medium heat and bring to a simmer. Turn the heat to low and simmer until syrupy, about 5 minutes. Remove the vanilla bean and scrape the seeds into the syrup. Discard the pod (or rinse and dry it and reserve for another use). Let the syrup cool completely, then add the blood orange sections. Cover and refrigerate for at least 1 hour, or up to 24 hours.

Run a sharp knife around the edges of each ramekin to break the suction, place a serving plate over the top, and invert so the panna cotta releases onto the plate. If it doesn't release, dip the bottom of the ramekin into hot water for a few seconds and try again. Garnish with the blood orange compote to serve.

SERVES 6

LEMON-GINGER ICEBOX CAKE

2½ cups [600 ml] whipping cream

½ cup [50 g] powdered sugar

1 cup [280 g] Lemon Curd (page 158)

About 50 ginger wafers (I use Anna's), plus more for garnish

Start to finish: 9 hours
Hands-on time: 1 hour

Beat the cream and powdered sugar in a mixer bowl on high speed until stiff peaks form, then fold in the lemon curd with a wide rubber spatula.

Arrange a single layer of cookies (about 12 cookies) in a circle on a serving plate, filling in the center with broken pieces. Spread a layer of the lemon cream over the top, then continue layering the remaining cookies and lemon cream. Crumble a few extra cookies and sprinkle over the top. Cover with plastic wrap and refrigerate for at least 8 hours, or up to 24 hours. Cut into slices and serve.

SERVES 8

When you need an easy make-ahead dessert, this icebox cake is your ace in the hole. The crispy ginger wafers absorb the moisture from the lemony cream, transforming overnight into a rich cake that's fit for a backyard barbecue or a fancy dinner with the boss. And it is so simple. Just whip up the lemon curd, beat the cream, and assemble. The next day you have a delectable masterpiece.

LEMON-ALMOND TRIFLE
WITH SUMMER BERRIES

Start to finish: 48 hours
Hands-on time: 2 hours

Colorfully layered in a peekaboo glass trifle bowl, this dessert tastes even better than it looks. The perfect make-ahead sweet for a special occasion, a trifle makes a beautiful centerpiece and is plentiful enough to satisfy a large dinner party. Every element of this dish is special, from the almond cake to the cream cheese filling, fresh berry purée, and lemon curd. This trifle has been known to elevate the baker to rock-star status, so be prepared when friends and family beg you to make it again and again.

ZESTY TIP

Bake the cake up to 3 days in advance and store, covered, at room temperature. Make the lemon syrup and store, covered, in the refrigerator for up to 3 days.

LEMON-ALMOND GENOISE

1 cup [120 g] unbleached all-purpose flour

½ tsp kosher salt

2 tsp baking powder

½ cup [60 g] finely ground blanched almonds

5 large eggs, separated, at room temperature

1 cup [200 g] sugar

Zest of 2 lemons, plus ¼ cup [60 ml] fresh lemon juice

1 tsp vanilla extract

1 tsp almond extract

LEMON SYRUP

1 cup [240 ml] water

1 cup [100 g] sugar

Zest of 1 lemon, plus ⅓ cup [80 ml] fresh lemon juice

CREAM CHEESE FILLING

8 oz [230 g] cream cheese, softened

¾ cup [150 g] sugar

2 cups [480 ml] heavy cream

½ tsp vanilla extract

1½ cups [220 g] blackberries

1 cup [120 g] blueberries

2 cups [560 g] Lemon Curd (page 158)

TO MAKE THE GENOISE: Preheat the oven to 350°F [180°C]. Grease a 15-by-10-by-1-in [38-by-25-by-2.5-cm] jelly-roll pan. Line the bottom with parchment paper, then grease and flour the parchment, knocking out the excess.

Sift the flour, salt, and baking powder into a small bowl, then whisk in the ground almonds. Set aside.

Beat the egg yolks, ¾ cup [150 g] of the sugar, and the lemon zest in a mixer bowl on high speed until thick and pale, about 4 minutes. Beat in the lemon juice, vanilla, and almond extract and continue beating for another 3 minutes, or until a ribbon forms when the beaters are lifted. Add the flour mixture and beat until combined. Set aside.

sweet and tart

continued

In another bowl and with clean beaters, beat the egg whites on high speed until soft peaks form, and then slowly beat in the remaining ¼ cup [50 g] sugar until stiff peaks form. Gently fold one-third of the whites into the batter with a wide rubber spatula to lighten it, and then fold in the remaining whites until no streaks remain.

Spread the batter evenly in the prepared pan. Bake for 15 to 20 minutes, or until the cake is golden and springs back when pressed lightly. Let cool in the pan on a wire rack for 5 minutes, then invert onto the rack and remove the parchment. Let the cake stand uncovered overnight to dry out. Cut into 1-in [2.5-cm] cubes.

TO MAKE THE SYRUP: Combine the water, sugar, lemon zest, and lemon juice in a small saucepan over medium heat and bring to a boil. Cook, stirring occasionally, until the sugar dissolves. Remove from the heat and let cool completely.

TO MAKE THE FILLING: Beat the cream cheese, ½ cup [100 g] of the sugar, and ½ cup [120 ml] of the cream in a mixer bowl on medium speed until smooth. In another large bowl, beat the remaining ¼ cup [50 g] sugar, remaining 1½ cups [360 ml] cream, and vanilla until stiff peaks form. Fold the whipped cream into the cream cheese mixture in two additions with a wide rubber spatula to lighten it.

Combine the blackberries and blueberries and dump two-thirds of them in a medium bowl. Add ⅓ cup [80 ml] of the lemon syrup and smash the berries to a purée with a potato masher (the mixture will still be chunky).

Place one-third of the cake cubes in the bottom of a large trifle dish and drizzle with about ⅓ cup [80 ml] of the remaining lemon syrup. Spoon one-third of the filling over the cubes and spread to the sides of the dish. Spoon half of the berry purée over and spread to the sides of the dish. Dollop half of the lemon curd over the purée and spread to the sides of the dish. Repeat the layering with half the remaining cake, ⅓ cup [80 ml] syrup, half the remaining filling, remaining berry purée, remaining cake, ⅓ cup [80 ml] syrup, remaining lemon curd, and remaining filling. Garnish with the whole berries. Cover and refrigerate overnight before serving.

SERVES 10 TO 12

CHILLED LEMON SOUFFLÉ
WITH LEMON SAUCE

Start to finish:
3 hours, 40 minutes
Hands-on time: 40 minutes

Soufflés make a grand gesture. Rising above the rim of the soufflé dish, they look daunting but are surprisingly easy to make if you have a stand mixer and a couple of mixer bowls. This lemony rendition is especially smart, as some of the sabayon (egg yolk and lemon mixture) is reserved to use as a sauce for the finished dessert.

2½ tsp unflavored gelatin

¼ cup [60 ml] cold water

7 large eggs, separated, at room temperature

1½ cups [300 g] sugar, plus 2 Tbsp

Zest of 2 lemons, plus ¾ cup [180 ml] fresh lemon juice

Pinch of kosher salt

1½ cups [360 ml] heavy cream

Cut a piece of parchment paper or aluminum foil long enough to fit around a 6-cup [1.4-L] soufflé dish and fold so it is about 5 in [12 cm] high. Brush the inside of the collar with vegetable oil, and tie the collar to the dish with kitchen string or a very large rubber band so that the collar extends 2 in [5 cm] above the rim of the dish.

Sprinkle the gelatin over the ¼ cup [60 ml] water in a medium heat-proof bowl and let soften for 5 minutes.

Whisk the egg yolks, 1½ cups [300 g] sugar, lemon zest, lemon juice, and salt in a heavy saucepan over medium heat and cook, stirring with a heat-proof spatula, for about 4 minutes, or until the mixture just begins to thicken. Be careful not to boil or the eggs will curdle. Transfer the lemon mixture to a large heat-proof bowl and stir for a few minutes to stop the cooking. Remove about ⅓ cup [80 ml] of the mixture to use as a sauce, cover, and refrigerate until ready to serve, or up to 2 days.

Place the softened gelatin in a microwave and heat for 10 seconds, then stir it and heat for another 10 seconds. The gelatin should be melted. Alternatively, place the bowl in a saucepan of simmering water and stir until the graininess has dissolved. Add the gelatin to the hot lemon mixture.

Whip the egg whites in a mixer bowl on high speed until soft peaks form. Add the 2 Tbsp sugar and beat until firm peaks form.

Beat the cream in another mixer bowl on high speed until thick and it holds its shape.

Add ice and cold water to a large bowl and nestle the bowl with the lemon mixture in the ice bath. Stir until cool. Using a large spatula, gently but thoroughly fold in the egg whites and then the whipped cream. (Allowing the gelatin to set slightly over the chilled water will keep the soufflé from separating as it chills.) Spoon the soufflé into the prepared dish and smooth the top. Cover and refrigerate until set, at least 3 hours, or up to 2 days.

Remove the collar before serving the soufflé on pretty plates or in cups with a dollop of the chilled lemon sauce.

SERVES 8

WILLIAM'S FROZEN LEMON PIE

Start to finish: 5 hours
Hands-on time: 30 minutes

Growing up in West Virginia didn't offer much in the way of destination restaurants, but my grandfather's golf club (Williams Country Club in Weirton, West Virginia) served our favorite dessert ever—frozen lemon pie. Four generations of my family have enjoyed this rich, lemony, tart pie and now you can, as well.

2 cups [250 g] graham cracker crumbs

⅓ cup [65 g] granulated sugar

½ cup [110 g] unsalted butter, melted

2 pinches of kosher salt

Two 14-oz [396-g] cans sweetened condensed milk

5 egg yolks

Zest of 2 lemons, plus 1 cup plus 2 Tbsp [270 ml] fresh lemon juice

1 cup [240 ml] heavy cream

¼ cup [30 g] powdered sugar

½ tsp vanilla extract

Preheat the oven to 350°F [180°C].

Combine the graham cracker crumbs, granulated sugar, butter, and a pinch of salt in a medium bowl and toss with a fork until combined.

Dump the crumb mixture into a 9-in [23-cm] springform pan with removable sides and, using the bottom of a glass or measuring cup, press the crumbs on the bottom and about 1½ in [4 cm] up the sides of the pan. Bake for about 15 minutes, or until the crust just begins to brown. Let cool completely on a wire rack. Turn the oven temperature to 325°F [165°C].

Meanwhile, whisk the condensed milk, egg yolks, lemon zest, lemon juice, and remaining pinch of salt in a medium bowl. Pour the filling into the cooled crust and place on a baking sheet. Bake for about 30 minutes, or until set but still jiggly. Let cool completely on the wire rack. Cover with plastic wrap (do not let the plastic touch the top of the pie) and freeze for at least 4 hours, or up to 1 week.

Up to 2 hours before serving, whip the cream, powdered sugar, and vanilla in a mixer bowl on high speed until thick and the whipped cream holds its shape. Cover and refrigerate.

When ready to serve, release the sides of the pan and slice with a knife that's been warmed in a glass of hot water. For neat slices, dip and wipe the knife with a paper towel after each cut. Top each slice with a dollop of whipped cream.

SERVES 8

MEYER LEMON ICE CREAM

Start to finish: 9 hours
Hands-on time: 30 minutes

Making your own ice cream is really easy, and the results are worth every minute of the wait for it to freeze. Zippy lemon ice cream is especially charming because it is at once bracingly tart yet creamy and smooth. I searched hard for the perfect balance here—just enough cream to be delicious, but not over-the-top rich.

1½ cups [360 ml] heavy cream

Zest of 3 Meyer lemons, plus ⅓ cup [80 ml] fresh Meyer lemon juice

1 vanilla bean, split lengthwise

1 cup [200 g] sugar

¼ tsp kosher salt

6 egg yolks

2 cups [480 ml] whole milk

Combine the cream, lemon zest, and vanilla bean in a large saucepan over medium-high heat and bring to a simmer. Remove from the heat and, with a slotted spoon, transfer the vanilla bean halves to a cutting board. Using the flat side of a knife, run the blade down the length of the bean to remove the seeds. Add the seeds and vanilla pod to the cream, cover, and let steep for 20 minutes to allow the flavors to develop.

Whisk the sugar, salt, egg yolks, and lemon juice in a large heat-proof bowl until well blended.

Remove the vanilla pod and discard (or rinse and dry it and reserve for another use). Bring the cream back to a simmer over medium-high heat and slowly whisk it into the egg mixture. Pour it back into the pan and cook over medium heat, stirring constantly with a heat-proof spatula or wooden spoon, for 3 to 4 minutes, or until the custard begins to thicken and coats the back of the spatula. Remove from the heat and stir in the milk.

Transfer the custard to a bowl and chill until cold, at least 4 hours or up to overnight. Transfer to an ice-cream maker and churn according to the manufacturer's instructions. Transfer the ice cream to a container, cover, and freeze until firm, at least 4 hours or up to 1 week, before serving.

MAKES ABOUT 1 QT [960 ML]

sweet
and tart

ORANGE SHERBET

8 sugar cubes

8 Valencia oranges

One 7-oz [200-g] envelope gelatin

1 cup [200 g] granulated sugar

2 cups [480 ml] skim milk

Start to finish: 9 hours
Hands-on time: 30 minutes

Rub the edges of the sugar cubes over the oranges so they pick up the oranges' zest and oils. (Some oranges give up their zest more easily than others. Don't worry if the sugar cubes dissolve a little bit. They should turn bright orange.) Be careful not to rub too deeply into the white pith, which can transfer a bitter edge to your sherbet. Set aside.

Juice the oranges with a citrus juicer or squeeze them by hand with a reamer. Combine the juice and sugar cubes in a medium saucepan. Sprinkle the gelatin over the orange juice and let soften for 5 minutes.

Add the granulated sugar to the orange juice mixture and heat over medium heat, stirring until the gelatin and sugar have dissolved. Do not boil. Remove from the heat and stir in the milk (the mixture will look curdled).

Transfer the sherbet base to a bowl and chill until cold, at least 4 hours or up to overnight. Transfer to an ice-cream maker and churn according to the manufacturer's instructions. Transfer the sherbet to a container, cover, and freeze until firm, at least 4 hours or up to 1 week, before serving.

MAKES ABOUT 1 QT [960 ML]

Remember those tubs of orange sherbet your mom used to buy when you were a kid? This sherbet is nothing like that. For one thing, the bulk of the orange flavor comes from rubbing sugar cubes against the skin of an orange, an old-fashioned (but possibly the most brilliant) way to capture all the orange oil and transport it into this confection.

ZESTY TIP

Be sure to buy brightly colored, pebbly, thick-skinned oranges for this recipe. Thinner skins won't yield enough orange oil and will result in a disappointingly bland-flavored sherbet.

STRAWBERRY SORBET WITH LEMON

Start to finish: 8 hours
Hands-on time: 10 minutes

I think we love sorbet because it's lighter than ice cream and sherbet, but still packs a walloping punch of flavor. This strawberry sorbet is unique, as it contains every bit of a lemon half, plus the juice and zest from the other half. Even if your strawberries are the unremarkable, unseasonable February kind, this sorbet will knock your socks off.

1 lemon; ½ quartered, seeded, and roughly chopped, ½ zested and juiced

1 cup [200 g] sugar

3¾ cups [540 g] fresh strawberries, hulled

Combine the chopped lemon, lemon zest, lemon juice, and sugar in the bowl of a food processor and process for about 1 minute, or until finely ground. Add the strawberries and process for about 1 minute, or until smooth.

Transfer the sorbet base to a bowl and chill until cold, at least 4 hours or up to overnight. Transfer to an ice-cream maker and churn according to the manufacturer's instructions. Transfer the sorbet to a container, cover, and freeze until firm, at least 4 hours or up to 1 week, before serving.

MAKES ABOUT 3 CUPS [720 ML]

FROZEN LEMON KEFIR

3 cups [720 ml] kefir or
buttermilk

Zest of 2 lemons, plus ½ cup
[120 ml] fresh lemon juice

⅔ cup [220 g] honey

Pinch of kosher salt

Fresh blueberries or thin
butter cookies for serving
(optional)

Start to finish: 8 hours
Hands-on time: 20 minutes

Whisk the kefir, lemon zest, lemon juice, honey, and salt in
a medium bowl until blended.

Chill until cold, at least 4 hours or up to overnight. Transfer
to an ice-cream maker and churn according to the manufacturer's instructions. Transfer the frozen kefir to a container, cover, and freeze until firm, at least 4 hours, or up
to 1 week, before serving. Accompany with a handful of
blueberries or thin butter cookies, if desired.

MAKES ABOUT 1 QT [960 ML]

A number of years ago, I ran across
a recipe for lemon kefir ice cream on
Clotilde Dusoulier's website, Chocolate
& Zucchini, that looked so simple yet so
delicious, I had to try it immediately. The
fermented milk and lemon are brilliant
together, and all that was needed to make
it dessert was a little sweetener in the
form of honey. I was smitten.

MEYER LEMON AND BLACKBERRY ICES

Start to finish: 4 hours
Hands-on time: 30 minutes

Just the thing for a hot summer's day, this light-as-a-feather lemon ice becomes something special when paired with the intense flavor of blackberry. I don't know which is more captivating, the taste or the color.

One of the most attractive features of a summer ice is the fact that you don't need an ice-cream maker to freeze it. I usually make fruit ice a day ahead just to be sure it is firm; but even slushy, these fruit ices are heaven.

ZESTY TIP

Charming Meyer lemons aren't as puckery as regular lemons. They are thought to be a cross between a lemon and a mandarin orange, and taste as if that might be true. If you can't find them, go ahead and use regular lemons—but up the sugar to 1 cup [200 g]. Blueberries can stand in for the blackberries with no change to the recipe. Another nice way to incorporate these ices into a menu is to pour a shot of vodka or tequila over them and serve as a cocktail of sorts. Or a boozy dessert. Both work for me.

MEYER LEMON ICE

2 cups [480 ml] water

¾ cup [150 g] sugar

Pinch of kosher salt

¾ cup [180 ml] fresh Meyer lemon juice

BLACKBERRY ICE

5 cups [725 g] blackberries

½ cup [120 ml] water

¾ cup [260 g] honey

2 Tbsp fresh lemon juice

Pinch of kosher salt

TO MAKE THE LEMON ICE: Combine the water, sugar, and salt in a medium saucepan over medium-high heat and bring to a simmer, stirring until the sugar is dissolved. Remove from the heat and stir in the lemon juice. Let cool to room temperature.

TO MAKE THE BLACKBERRY ICE: Combine the blackberries and water in a blender or the bowl of a food processor. Process for about 30 seconds, or until well blended. Strain the berry mixture through a medium-mesh strainer into a bowl, pressing the liquid through with a rubber spatula in three or four batches. Stir in the honey, lemon juice, and salt.

Pour the mixtures into two separate 9-by-13-in [23-by-33-cm] pans. Place in the freezer for 1 hour. Remove the pans from the freezer and scrape the frozen edges into the center of the pans with a fork. Return to the freezer for 1 hour. Scrape the ice crystals again to the center and return to the freezer for at least 1 hour, or up to overnight. Store the ices in the freezer for up to 3 days, covered. If they become too firm to scoop, scrape again with the tines of a fork to loosen the crystals. Place one scoop of each ice into chilled bowls to serve.

MAKES ABOUT 1 QT [960 ML]

CHAPTER 5

MUFFINS, SCONES, AND BREAKFAST BREADS

Nothing wakes up your mouth like the tang of citrus, so why not get a jump-start on the day by waking up with one of these zingy breakfast options? Whether made in advance or baked fresh on a weekend morning, sunny breads are sure to brighten everyone's day.

LEMONY BLUEBERRY MUFFINS
WITH LEMON STREUSEL

Start to finish: 1 hour
Hands-on time: 20 minutes

Blueberry-packed muffins make almost everyone swoon. Add some zesty lemon and you've got the perfect antidote to waking up in the morning.

ZESTY TIP

Tossing the blueberries with flour helps to keep the juices from bleeding out into the muffin, preventing gumminess. I've loaded this muffin with blueberries to the max, so don't omit this step.

MUFFINS

2 cups [240 g] unbleached all-purpose flour, plus 1 Tbsp

2 tsp baking powder

½ tsp kosher salt

¾ cup [150 g] granulated sugar

Zest of 2 lemons, plus 3 Tbsp fresh lemon juice

½ cup [110 g] unsalted butter, softened

2 large eggs, at room temperature

½ cup [120 ml] whole milk

3½ cups [525 g] fresh or thawed frozen blueberries

STREUSEL TOPPING

½ cup [60 g] unbleached all-purpose flour

¼ cup [50 g] firmly packed light brown sugar

3 Tbsp unsalted butter, softened

Zest of 1 lemon

TO MAKE THE MUFFINS: Preheat the oven to 375°F [190°C]. Grease a 12-cup muffin pan or line with paper cups.

Whisk the 2 cups [240 g] flour, baking powder, and salt in a medium bowl until combined. Set aside.

Beat the granulated sugar, lemon zest, and butter in a mixer bowl on medium speed until light and fluffy. Add the eggs, one at a time, scraping down the sides of the bowl after each addition. Beat in the milk and lemon juice. Turn the speed to low and add the flour mixture in three additions, beating until just combined.

Gently toss the blueberries with the 1 Tbsp flour in a small bowl, then gently fold them into the batter with a large rubber spatula. Divide the batter evenly among the prepared muffin cups using a ¼-cup [60-ml] scoop.

sweet
and tart

TO MAKE THE TOPPING: Combine the flour, brown sugar, butter, and lemon zest in a medium bowl and mix with your fingers, rubbing in the butter until crumbly.

Sprinkle the streusel over the tops of the muffins. Bake for 25 to 30 minutes, or until golden brown. Let cool in the pan on a wire rack for 10 minutes, then turn out onto the rack to finish cooling. Eat within a few hours or store, tightly wrapped, in the freezer for up to 4 weeks. Thaw at room temperature and rewarm in a 300°F [150°C] oven for 10 minutes.

MAKES 12 MUFFINS

LEMONY BISCUITS
WITH ASSORTED FILLINGS

Start to finish: 30 minutes
Hands-on time: 15 minutes

Southern cooking teacher and award-winning cookbook author Shirley Corriher taught me how to make her trademark biscuits many years ago. I've fooled around with her ratios and technique (shame on me), but I think she'd enjoy these buttery, flaky, lemon-infused biscuits. They're fabulous for breakfast with lemon curd or jam, or used to sandwich together bacon, ham, and/or fried green tomatoes.

2 cups [240 g] unbleached all-purpose flour

3 Tbsp sugar

2 tsp baking powder

1 tsp baking soda

½ tsp kosher salt

Grated zest of 2 lemons

½ cup plus 2 Tbsp [135 g] cold unsalted butter, cubed; plus 2 Tbsp, melted

¾ cup [180 ml] buttermilk

SUGGESTED FILLINGS (OPTIONAL)

Lemon Curd (page 158)

Crispy bacon and pimiento cheese

Ham and apple butter

Fried green tomatoes and bacon

Preheat the oven to 425°F [220°C]. Grease a 9-in [23-cm] round cake pan.

Combine the flour, sugar, baking powder, baking soda, salt, and lemon zest in a large bowl. Add the ½ cup plus 2 Tbsp [140 g] butter and rub it in with your fingertips until no lumps of butter remain. Make a well in the center of the mixture and pour in the buttermilk, stirring with a wooden spoon or fork just until the dry ingredients are moistened. The dough will be very wet (do not overmix).

Turn the dough out onto a lightly floured work surface and sprinkle the top with flour. Pat into a round about ¾ in [2 cm] thick and cut out biscuits using a 2-in [5-cm] round cutter dipped in flour. Be careful not to twist the cutter or the biscuits won't rise as high. (The dough will be gooey and your hands will get messy, but this soft dough will yield the lightest biscuits.) Gather up the scraps, pat into a round about ¾ in [2 cm] thick, and cut out more biscuits.

sweet and tart

Transfer to the prepared pan, nestling the biscuits close together, and brush the tops with some of the melted butter.

Bake for 10 minutes, then rotate the pan 180 degrees and bake for another 7 minutes, or until the biscuits are lightly golden. Remove from the oven and brush the tops with the remaining melted butter.

Run a knife around the edge of the pan to loosen the biscuits and turn out onto a serving plate. Pull apart and serve hot, with fillings if desired. Store at room temperature for up to 2 hours (the biscuits do not keep well beyond that).

MAKES ABOUT 16 BISCUITS

LEMON SCONES
WITH BLACKBERRIES

Start to finish: 45 minutes
Hands-on time: 20 minutes

Once upon a time, I worked in a small bakery and made these scones every day. Ladies would come in and buy three or four at a time, quizzing us on the ingredients. Did we use buttermilk (low fat) or heavy cream in the scones? "Oh, we use buttermilk," we would say. They were so happy to indulge carefree in their little treat. They never asked about the large amount of butter, so we didn't bring it up. I still feel a little guilty about that.

But you definitely won't feel guilty about making and eating these buttery, flaky scones. They're light and airy and full of juicy blackberries with an addictively tart glaze—so good that you can't eat only one. Just ask the ladies.

2 cups [240 g] unbleached all-purpose flour

⅓ cup [65 g] granulated sugar

2 tsp baking powder

1 tsp baking soda

¼ tsp kosher salt

Zest of 1 lemon, plus 1 Tbsp fresh lemon juice

½ cup plus 2 Tbsp [135 g] unsalted butter, softened and cubed

⅔ cup [160 ml] buttermilk, plus 2 Tbsp

3½ cups [500 g] fresh blackberries

1 cup [100 g] powdered sugar

Preheat the oven to 400°F [200°C]. Line a baking sheet with parchment paper.

Combine the flour, granulated sugar, baking powder, baking soda, salt, and lemon zest in a large bowl. Add the butter and rub it in with your fingers until the mixture resembles fine meal. Stir in the ⅔ cup [160 ml] buttermilk and the blackberries just until combined.

Turn the dough out onto a lightly floured work surface and divide into two equal mounds. Sprinkle the top of each mound with a little flour and gently pat into a disk about 6 in [15 cm] in diameter. Cut each into six wedges.

Transfer the scones to the prepared baking sheet and brush the tops with the 2 Tbsp buttermilk. Bake for 25 to 30 minutes, or until golden brown and firm to the touch. Let cool slightly on the baking sheet on a wire rack.

continued

ZESTY TIPS

The trick to making light, flaky scones is to not overwork the dough. Rub the butter into the flour and then stir in the buttermilk just until the mixture is moistened fairly evenly. If you keep stirring until uniformly wet, the scones will be dense, heavy, and not nearly as delightful.

Freeze unbaked scones on parchment-lined baking sheets, then transfer the scones to freezer bags or wrap tightly in plastic wrap and freeze for up to 3 months. Thaw on parchment-lined baking sheets and bake as directed.

Combine the powdered sugar and lemon juice in a small bowl and blend with a fork to make a glaze. Drizzle the glaze over the warm scones. (If the glaze is too thick to drizzle, add a few drops of lemon juice or water.) Serve warm or at room temperature within a few hours after baking for the best flavor and texture. If you must make them ahead, let cool to room temperature, transfer to freezer bags, and store in the freezer for up to 2 months. Thaw at room temperature and rewarm in a 300°F [150°C] oven for 10 minutes.

MAKES 12 SCONES

sweet and tart

OLIVE OIL–POPPY SEED LOAF
WITH LEMON GLAZE

1½ cups [180 g] unbleached all-purpose flour

1½ tsp baking powder

¼ tsp baking soda

½ tsp kosher salt

1 cup [200 g] granulated sugar

Zest of 1 lemon; plus ¼ cup [60 ml] fresh lemon juice, plus 2 Tbsp

1 cup [240 ml] plain whole-milk Greek yogurt

3 large eggs, at room temperature

½ cup [120 ml] extra-virgin olive oil

1 Tbsp poppy seeds

¾ cup [90 g] powdered sugar

1 Tbsp heavy cream

Start to finish: 2 hours
Hands-on time: 30 minutes

I love this cake. It's rich, moist, and lemony, with a hint of olive oil flavor that takes you by surprise and charms you into eating another slice. Made with extra-virgin olive oil instead of butter, this loaf is kind of good for you. Really. Go ahead and enjoy another sliver.

Preheat the oven to 350°F [180°C]. Grease a 5-by-9-in [12-by-23-cm] loaf pan and line the bottom with parchment paper.

Whisk the flour, baking powder, baking soda, and salt in a medium bowl until combined. Set aside.

Beat the granulated sugar, lemon zest, ¼ cup [60 ml] lemon juice, and yogurt in a mixer bowl on medium speed until blended. Add the eggs, one at a time, and then the olive oil and beat until creamy. Turn the speed to low, add the flour mixture in three additions, and beat until smooth. Add the poppy seeds and beat until just blended.

Pour the batter into the prepared pan and smooth the top. Bake for about 1 hour, or until a wooden skewer inserted into the center comes out clean. Let cool in the pan on a wire rack for 15 minutes, then turn out onto the rack. Peel off the parchment and turn the loaf right-side up.

continued

Combine the powdered sugar, cream, and 2 Tbsp lemon juice in a small bowl and blend with a fork to make a glaze.

Place the rack with the warm cake on a baking sheet (to catch the drips). Poke holes in the top of the cake with the wooden skewer and pour half of the glaze over the top. Once the cake has cooled completely, pour the remaining glaze over the top and let it dry before slicing. Store, covered, at room temperature for up to 4 days.

SERVES 10

sweet
and tart

LEMON MONKEY BREAD

Start to finish:
3 hours, 30 minutes
Hands-on time: 45 minutes

Monkey bread just might give us a good enough reason to reinvent the kaffeeklatsch. Make this breakfast bread and serve it warm from the oven with strong, hot coffee—and linger at the table.

ZESTY TIP

You can assemble the bread but do not let it rise the second time. Cover with plastic wrap and refrigerate for up to 24 hours. Remove from the refrigerator, let rise (it will take a little longer as the dough is chilled), and bake as directed.

¼ cup [60 ml] warm (105° to 115°F [40° to 45°C]) water

⅓ cup [65 g] granulated sugar, plus ¾ cup [150 g]

Scant 1 Tbsp active dry yeast

1 cup [240 ml] warm (105° to 115°F [40° to 45°C]) milk

3 Tbsp unsalted butter, softened, plus ½ cup [110 g], melted

1 tsp kosher salt

1 large egg, at room temperature

Zest of 4 lemons, plus ¼ cup [60 ml] fresh lemon juice

3¾ cups [450 g] unbleached all-purpose flour

¾ cup [150 g] firmly packed light brown sugar

1 tsp lemon oil

2 cups [200 g] powdered sugar

Combine the warm water and a pinch of granulated sugar in a large mixer bowl. Sprinkle the yeast over the top and let stand for 5 minutes, or until foamy.

Add the warm milk, ⅓ cup [65 g] granulated sugar, 3 Tbsp softened butter, salt, egg, and three-fourths of the lemon zest to the yeast mixture. Using the paddle attachment on a stand mixer, beat on low speed until incorporated, or mix with a wooden spoon. Add the flour 1 cup [120 g] at a time and switch to the dough hook when the dough starts to become stiff after the second addition of flour. If mixing by hand, continue stirring with the wooden spoon. Knead the dough with the dough hook on low speed for about 1 minute, or turn the dough out onto a work surface and knead with your hands until the dough is smooth.

Transfer the dough to a clean bowl and cover with plastic wrap. Let rise in a warm place for about 1 hour, or until doubled.

sweet
and tart

Combine the brown sugar and ¾ cup [150 g] granulated sugar in a large, shallow bowl. Combine the ½ cup [110 g] melted butter and lemon oil in another large, shallow bowl.

Grease a 10-in [25-cm] Bundt pan.

Roll the dough into a log about 26 in [66 cm] long and cut into about twenty-two golf ball–size pieces. Roll into balls and coat in the melted butter mixture, then roll in the sugar mixture. Layer them next to and on top of each other in the prepared pan. Sprinkle the remaining butter and sugar mixtures on top. Cover with plastic wrap and let rise in a warm place for about 1 hour, or until doubled.

Preheat the oven to 350°F [180°C].

Remove the plastic wrap and bake for about 30 minutes, or until the monkey bread is browned and puffy. Let cool in the pan on a wire rack for 15 minutes, then turn out onto a serving platter and let cool for 15 minutes.

Meanwhile, combine the powdered sugar, lemon juice, and remaining lemon zest in a small bowl and blend with a fork to make a glaze. Drizzle the glaze over the warm bread and serve.

MAKES ONE 10-IN [25-CM] LOAF

muffins, 125 scones, and breakfast breads

LEMON SWEET ROLLS
WITH FRANGIPANE AND CREAM CHEESE ICING

Start to finish: 5 hours
Hands-on time: 45 minutes

When I was a little girl, my mom would make those Pillsbury packaged sweet rolls that you freed from the can by whacking it on the edge of the laminate countertop. We loved the whole scenario, hot sweet rolls and all . . . but looking back on it, I think the whacking was the best part.

Eating is the best part of these sunny sweet rolls filled with almond frangipane and slathered with cream cheese icing. Sorry, Mom. These are way better.

ZESTY TIP

You can shape the rolls and place in the pan, but do not let rise the second time. Cover with plastic wrap and refrigerate overnight. Remove from the refrigerator, let rise (it will take a little longer as the dough is chilled), and bake as directed. Or freeze the unbaked rolls for up to 4 weeks, thaw at room temperature, let rise, and bake.

DOUGH

3 cups [360 g] unbleached all-purpose flour

1 tsp kosher salt

¼ cup [60 ml] lukewarm (105° to 115°F [40° to 45°C]) milk

Scant 1 Tbsp active dry yeast

¼ cup [50 g] granulated sugar

3 large eggs, at room temperature

Zest of 2 lemons

¾ cup [170 g] unsalted butter, softened and cubed

FRANGIPANE

1½ cups [180 g] blanched almonds

½ cup [100 g] granulated sugar

6 Tbsp [85 g] unsalted butter, softened

¼ cup [30 g] unbleached all-purpose flour

2 large eggs, at room temperature

1 tsp almond extract

Pinch of kosher salt

ICING

4 oz [115 g] cream cheese, softened

2 cups [200 g] powdered sugar

2 Tbsp heavy cream

Zest of 1 lemon, plus 1 Tbsp fresh lemon juice

Line a 9-by-13-in [23-by-33-cm] baking pan with parchment paper, letting the excess hang over the sides of the pan. (The overhang will help you to lift the rolls from the pan.)

TO MAKE THE DOUGH: Whisk the flour and salt in a small bowl. Set aside.

Pour the warm milk into a small bowl. Sprinkle the yeast over the top and let stand for 5 minutes, or until foamy.

Combine the granulated sugar, eggs, and lemon zest in a mixer bowl. Using the paddle attachment on a stand mixer, beat on medium speed, or mix with a wooden spoon. Turn the speed to low and beat in the yeast mixture until blended, or mix in with the spoon.

sweet
and tart

Using the dough hook attachment, add the flour mixture in three additions and beat on low speed until incorporated, or mix with the spoon. The dough will be stiff. If using a stand mixer, beat in the butter one piece at a time on low speed. Continue to beat until the butter is completely incorporated, scraping down the sides of the bowl as necessary. If mixing by hand, it will be easier to mix in the butter with your fingers. Turn the dough out onto a lightly floured work surface and knead with your hands for about 5 minutes, or until smooth and satiny.

Transfer the dough to a clean bowl and cover with a towel. Let rise in a warm place for about 2 hours, or until doubled.

MEANWHILE, MAKE THE FRANGIPANE: Combine the almonds and granulated sugar in the bowl of a food processor and process until finely ground. Add the butter, flour, eggs, almond extract, and salt and pulse until well mixed. The frangipane should be thick.

When the dough has risen, roll out on a lightly floured work surface into a rectangle about 18 by 11 in [46 by 28 cm]. Spread the frangipane evenly over the dough, leaving a 1-in [2.5-cm] border uncovered. Starting from one long end, roll up the dough and pinch the long edge to seal. Cut into twelve equal pieces.

Place the rolls, cut-side up, in the prepared pan in rows of three. Cover with plastic wrap and let rise in a warm place for about 1½ hours, or until doubled.

continued

Preheat the oven to 350°F [180°C].

Remove the plastic wrap and bake the rolls for about 35 minutes, or until golden brown. Let cool in the pan on a wire rack for 10 minutes, then remove from the pan and let cool on the rack for about 20 minutes.

MEANWHILE, MAKE THE ICING: Beat the cream cheese, powdered sugar, cream, lemon zest, and lemon juice in a mixer bowl on medium speed until a thick, spreadable icing forms; it should be spreadable but not too thin. (If it is too thick, add a few drops of water; if it is too thin, add more powdered sugar.)

Spread the icing over the rolls. Serve warm or at room temperature. They are best eaten within a few hours of baking.

MAKES 12 ROLLS

sweet and tart

MINI GINGER DONUTS
WITH LEMON GLAZE

2½ cups [300 g] unbleached all-purpose flour

2 Tbsp cornstarch

1 Tbsp ground ginger

2 tsp baking powder

1 tsp kosher salt

½ tsp baking soda

Pinch of freshly grated nutmeg

¾ cup [150 g] granulated sugar

1 large egg

½ cup [120 ml] buttermilk

4 Tbsp [55 g] unsalted butter, melted

1 tsp vanilla extract

Zest of 2 lemons, plus ¼ cup [60 ml] fresh lemon juice

½ cup [90 g] chopped candied ginger

Vegetable oil for deep-frying

2 cups [200 g] powdered sugar

Start to finish: 3 hours
Hands-on time: 1 hour

Everybody has their weakness, and donuts are my kryptonite. But just any ol' donut won't do. Since the most delicious donuts are super-fresh, I've found that the best are the ones I make myself. Plus, I can create them in flavors I would never find at a donut shop, like the lemony, spicy ginger ones here. Fry them up once and you will definitely fry them up again.

Whisk the flour, cornstarch, ground ginger, baking powder, salt, baking soda, and nutmeg in a large bowl until combined. Set aside.

Beat the granulated sugar and egg in a mixer bowl on high speed until light, about 3 minutes. Turn the speed to low and beat in the buttermilk, melted butter, vanilla, lemon zest, and ¼ cup [45 g] of the candied ginger. Slowly add half of the flour mixture and beat until combined. Remove the bowl from the mixer, add the remaining flour mixture, and mix by hand with a wooden spoon. The dough will be stiff. Cover the bowl and refrigerate for at least 2 hours, or up to overnight.

Pour vegetable oil into a cast-iron skillet to a depth of 2 in [5 cm] and heat to 350°F [180°C] on a deep-frying thermometer. Line a baking sheet with paper towels or brown paper bags (like you get at the grocery store).

continued

Roll out the dough on a lightly floured work surface to a thickness of ½ in [12 mm]. Cut out the donuts using a 2-in [5-cm] donut cutter, or use a 2-in [5-cm] round cutter and then cut out the centers using a ¾-in [2-cm] round cutter. Gather up the scraps, roll them out again, and cut out more donuts. (Be careful not to use too much flour or they will be tough.)

Fry six donuts at a time in the hot oil for about 1 minute, or until brown on one side. Carefully flip them over and fry for another minute. Remove with a slotted spoon or tongs and drain on the paper-lined baking sheet. Repeat to fry the remaining donuts. Let cool slightly.

Combine the powdered sugar and lemon juice in a small bowl and blend with a fork to make a glaze. Dip the tops of the doughnuts into the glaze and immediately sprinkle with the remaining ¼ cup [45 g] candied ginger. Eat within a few hours of frying.

MAKES ABOUT 24 MINI DONUTS

sweet
and tart

CRÊPES
WITH LIMONCELLO AND VANILLA CARAMELIZED PINEAPPLE

Start to finish: 2 hours
Hands-on time: 1 hour

Light and airy crêpes are a favorite of the make-ahead brunch dish crowd. Filled with caramelized pineapple spears and flecks of vanilla bean, these limoncello-spiked crêpes make a perfect ending to a meal, as well as a beginning to a day.

ZESTY TIP

You can cook the crêpes in advance, layer between sheets of parchment, and wrap, then freeze for up to 4 weeks. Thaw overnight in the refrigerator. Or, cook the crêpes 1 day ahead, wrap in the same way, and refrigerate. Warm them, wrapped, in a microwave. The pineapple can be cooked and refrigerated up to 24 hours ahead (reheat before using). The ricotta can be mixed up to 30 minutes ahead and kept at room temperature. Warm up the ricotta mixture in the microwave before assembling and serving the crêpes.

1 cup [120 g] unbleached all-purpose flour

¾ cup [150 g] granulated sugar

Pinch of kosher salt

3 large eggs, at room temperature

Zest of 2 lemons

2 Tbsp limoncello

6 Tbsp [85 g] unsalted butter; 2 Tbsp, melted

1½ cups [360 ml] whole milk

2 Tbsp vegetable oil

1 ripe pineapple, peeled, cored, and cut into 12 spears

1 vanilla bean, split lengthwise

1 cup [230 g] whole-milk ricotta cheese

Powdered sugar for garnish

Whisk the flour, ¼ cup [50 g] of the granulated sugar, and the salt in a medium bowl until combined. Whisk the eggs, half of the lemon zest, the limoncello, melted butter, and milk in another medium bowl until combined. Slowly whisk the egg mixture into the flour mixture and continue whisking until the batter is the consistency of thin cream. Let stand at room temperature for 1 to 2 hours before cooking the crêpes.

Heat a crêpe pan (6 in [15 cm] or 10 in [25 cm], according to desired size of crêpes) or a nonstick skillet over medium heat and carefully rub the pan bottom with a paper towel dipped into the vegetable oil. When the pan is hot, pour in about 3 Tbsp of the batter and immediately tilt the pan to cover the bottom in a thin layer. Cook for about 1 minute, or until no longer shiny on top and the edges are firm. Flip the crêpe over with a thin-edged spatula (or your fingers, if you're brave) and brown the other side, about 30 seconds. Transfer to a platter and cover with aluminum foil. Repeat to cook the remaining crêpes, oiling the pan before cooking each one.

continued

Melt the remaining 4 Tbsp [55 g] butter in a large skillet over medium-high heat. When hot, add the pineapple, vanilla bean, and ¼ cup [50 g] granulated sugar. Cook the pineapple for about 4 minutes, or until browned on one side, then flip the spears over and brown the other side. As the vanilla bean heats up, it will soften and the seeds will escape. With a slotted spoon, transfer the vanilla bean halves to a cutting board. Using the flat side of a knife, run the blade down the length of the bean to remove the seeds. Add the seeds to the pan. Discard the pod (or rinse and dry it and reserve for other use). Cook for another 2 minutes to infuse the flavor of the vanilla. The sugar will caramelize a bit; don't let it get too brown or it will harden as it cools. (If this happens, the juices from the pineapple will thin it down if you let it sit for an hour or so.)

Stir together the ricotta, remaining ¼ cup [55 g] granulated sugar, and remaining lemon zest in a small microwave-safe bowl and warm in the microwave for about 30 seconds.

Lay a warm crêpe on a heated plate and top with a dollop of sweetened ricotta, a pineapple spear, and a drizzle of the pan juices. Roll it up halfway, fold in the ends, and continue rolling the crêpe into a cylinder. Sprinkle with powdered sugar and serve warm.

MAKES ABOUT 12 CRÊPES

LEMON PAIN PERDU
WITH PLUM COMPOTE

4 large eggs

½ cup [120 ml] heavy cream

¾ cup [180 ml] whole milk

3 Tbsp firmly packed light brown sugar, plus ½ cup [100 g]

1 tsp vanilla extract

Zest of 2 lemons, plus ¼ cup [60 ml] fresh lemon juice

¼ tsp kosher salt

½ cup [110 g] unsalted butter, plus more for serving

6 plums, pitted and thinly sliced

8 slices challah or brioche, sliced ½ in [12 mm] thick

Powdered sugar for garnish

Start to finish: 45 minutes

Hands-on time: 45 minutes

Pain perdu (French toast) isn't just for breakfast—I have happily eaten it for lunch, dinner, and dessert, as well. It's especially delish when made with rich, eggy bread and paired with this tart plum compote, and is a great way to wake up, nosh, dine, or end the day. The ingredients for *pain perdu*, or "lost bread," are probably sitting in your kitchen as we speak . . . *n'est-ce pas?*

ZESTY TIP

You can make the plum compote and let cool, then cover and refrigerate for up to 3 days. Prepare the egg mixture, cover, and refrigerate for up to 1 day.

Whisk the eggs, cream, milk, 3 Tbsp brown sugar, vanilla, half of the lemon zest, and the salt in a large, shallow bowl. Set aside.

Heat a large skillet over medium-high heat and melt 2 Tbsp of the butter. When it sizzles, add the plums and cook for about 4 minutes, or until they begin to give off their juice. Add the ½ cup [100 g] brown sugar, lemon juice, and remaining lemon zest and cook for about 5 minutes, or until the plums are soft and syrupy. Remove from the heat and cover to keep warm.

Preheat the oven to 150°F [65°C].

Heat another large skillet over medium-high heat and melt 2 Tbsp butter. Working in batches, immerse the bread into the egg mixture so that it's good and saturated. Add to the skillet and cook for about 3 minutes on each side, or until browned. Transfer the French toast to a baking sheet and keep warm in the oven. Cook the remaining bread in batches using the remaining 4 Tbsp [55 g] butter.

Serve the French toast on heated plates, dab the tops with a pat of butter, and dust with powdered sugar. Ladle the warm plum compote over the top.

SERVES 4

muffins, 135 scones, and breakfast breads

CHAPTER 6
SAVORIES

There's a special place for lemon flavor in appetizers, or sides, or accompaniments to a soup, salad, or other light lunch. Lemon wakes up the palate and makes us salivate for whatever other tasty morsels are to be had. So here they are . . . breads, savory tarts, dips, and nibbles to get your party started.

MARINATED OLIVES
WITH LEMON AND ROSEMARY

Start to finish:
3 hours, 30 minutes
Hands-on time: 30 minutes

Quick and easy to pull together, this olive mélange gets its appeal from a lemony Provençal vinaigrette. Try to buy olives in a variety of colors and shapes, and don't worry about the pits. The olives will be much prettier and keep their shape if left whole.

ZESTY TIP

Leave a plate beside the bowl of olives with a few olive pits on it so guests will know where to dispose of them.

1 cup [240 ml] extra-virgin olive oil

2 garlic cloves, minced

2 Tbsp minced red onion

2 tsp fennel seeds

¼ tsp red pepper flakes

2 sprigs fresh rosemary

1 red bell pepper, seeded, deribbed, and cut into matchsticks

1 cup [130 g] Kalamata olives, drained

1 cup [130 g] Niçoise olives, drained

1 cup [130 g] Picholine olives, drained

Zest of 2 lemons, plus ¼ cup [60 ml] fresh lemon juice

2 Tbsp fresh basil leaves, thinly sliced

2 Tbsp minced fresh flat-leaf parsley

Heat the olive oil in a large skillet over medium heat. When the oil is hot, add the garlic, onion, fennel seeds, red pepper flakes, rosemary, and bell pepper. Cook for 1 minute, then add all the olives and sauté for 3 minutes. Remove from the heat. Let stand at room temperature for about 1 hour. Transfer to a bowl, cover, and refrigerate for at least 2 hours, or up to 1 week.

Just before serving, remove the rosemary sprigs and discard. Add the lemon zest, lemon juice, basil, and parsley and toss to mix. Bring to room temperature before serving in a decorative bowl.

MAKES ABOUT 3 CUPS [390 G]

sweet and tart

LEMONY HAZELNUT AND PARMESAN COOKIES
WITH THYME

1 cup [120 g] hazelnuts, toasted and skinned (see Zesty Tip)

2 cups [240 g] unbleached all-purpose flour

1½ cups [120 g] grated Parmesan cheese

1 cup [220 g] cold unsalted butter, cubed

2 Tbsp sugar

1 Tbsp fresh thyme leaves or 1 tsp dried

Kosher salt and freshly ground pepper

2 large eggs

¼ cup [60 ml] lemon oil

Start to finish: 3 hours
Hands-on time: 30 minutes

Pulse the cooled hazelnuts in the bowl of a food processor until finely ground. Add the flour, Parmesan, butter, sugar, thyme, 1 tsp salt, a few grinds of pepper, and the eggs and process until the dough comes together in a ball.

Transfer the dough to a lightly floured work surface and shape into a log about 2 in [5 cm] thick. Center it on a sheet of parchment paper and roll so it is as uniformly round as possible. Enclose the dough in the parchment and refrigerate until firm, about 2 hours.

Preheat the oven to 350°F [180°C]. Line two baking sheets with parchment paper.

Unwrap the log and cut into slices about ½ in [12 mm] thick. Transfer to the prepared baking sheets, spacing the cookies about 1 in [2.5 cm] apart. Brush with the lemon oil and sprinkle with salt. Bake for about 20 minutes, or until lightly golden around the edges and bottoms, rotating the baking sheets 180 degrees about halfway through the baking time. Let cool completely on the baking sheets on wire racks. Store, covered, at room temperature for up to 1 day. Serve at room temperature.

MAKES ABOUT 32 COOKIES

If you want to feel like a brilliant hostess, hide away a log of these cookies in your freezer. That way, the next time you pop a bottle of Champagne in honor of a friend's engagement, a nomination for an Academy Award, or even a cavity-free dentist appointment, all you have to do is slice and bake. The Parmesan and hazelnuts are addictive on their own, but the brush of lemon oil and sprinkle of salt on top take these savory cookies to a new level.

ZESTY TIP

To toast hazelnuts, spread in a single layer on a baking sheet and bake at 350°F [180°C] for about 5 minutes, or until the skins begin to loosen and the light nut underneath looks golden. Dump the nuts on a kitchen towel and wrap them up so they steam for a few minutes. Rub vigorously and then pick the skinned nuts from the towel, discarding the skins.

To make the dough in advance and then bake the cookies at a later date, see Zesty Tip, page 28.

LEMON, PEPPER, AND ASIAGO CRACKERS

Start to finish:
1 hour, 30 minutes
Hands-on time: 1 hour

It might seem crazy to make your own crackers when there are so many to choose from in the grocery store, but these crispy shingles are incredibly beguiling with their rustic, homemade charm. Pair them with a little local goat cheese and olives, and call it the only appetizer you'll ever need to make. If you'd like to serve them with a dip, don't opt for anything firmer than hummus, as the crackers are fragile.

1¾ cups [210 g] unbleached all-purpose flour

⅓ cup [65 g] sugar

1 tsp freshly ground pepper

½ tsp kosher salt

½ tsp baking powder

½ cup [110 g] cold unsalted butter, cubed

½ cup [40 g] grated Asiago cheese

1 large egg

Zest of 2 lemons, plus 1 Tbsp fresh lemon juice

1 Tbsp whole milk

Specialty sea salt such as Maldon, pink Himalayan, or black Hawaiian

3 Tbsp black sesame seeds (optional)

Preheat the oven to 350°F [180°C]. Line four baking sheets with parchment paper.

Combine the flour, sugar, pepper, kosher salt, and baking powder in the bowl of a food processor and pulse to combine. Add the butter and Asiago and process until they are cut into the flour and the mixture resembles coarse meal, about 20 pulses. Add the egg, lemon zest, and lemon juice and process until the dough comes together in a ball.

Turn the dough out onto a lightly floured work surface and shape into a log about 12 in [30.5 cm] long. Cut into 12 pieces. Keep the dough covered with plastic wrap so it doesn't dry out.

Flatten out one piece of dough on the work surface. Using a pasta roller, feed the dough through the rollers set on the widest setting (the dough will become very long). Place on one of the prepared baking sheets. Repeat to roll out the remaining dough, refrigerating each baking sheet as it fills up. (You can also roll out the dough using a rolling pin, but the crackers won't be quite as thin and crispy.)

Brush the milk over the tops of the dough and sprinkle lightly with sea salt and the sesame seeds (if using). Bake for about 20 minutes, or until the crackers are firm and brown. If you are baking more than one sheet at a time, rotate them 180 degrees about halfway through the baking time. Let cool on the baking sheets on wire racks. The crackers will crisp up as they cool. Break the crackers into the desired size. Store in sealable plastic bags at room temperature for up to 1 day.

MAKES TWELVE 4-BY-12-IN [10-BY-30.5-CM] CRACKERS

FLAT BREAD
WITH LEMONY PESTO AND RICOTTA

Start to finish:
3 hours, 30 minutes
Hands-on time: 30 minutes

On chilly nights with a pot of soup bubbling on the stove, we crave a freshly made bread hot from the oven to go with. It doesn't take much time to pull together this pretty, piquant, and meltingly delicious flat bread if you have the pesto in the fridge (you should always have pesto in the fridge), and it really rounds out a liquid meal. Now repeat after me: dip, slurp, tear, bite, dip, slurp . . . ahhh.

ZESTY TIP

If you must make the bread ahead, let it cool completely, wrap in aluminum foil, and freeze for up to 2 weeks. When ready to serve, thaw at room temperature and reheat in the foil in a 350°F [180°C] oven for about 5 minutes.

1⅓ cups [320 ml] warm (105° to 115°F [40° to 45°C]) water

Scant 1 Tbsp active dry yeast

1 tsp sugar

5 Tbsp [80 ml] extra-virgin olive oil

Kosher salt

Zest of 2 lemons, plus 2 tsp fresh lemon juice

3 cups [360 g] unbleached all-purpose flour

½ cup [110 g] Lemony Basil Pesto (page 164)

Freshly ground pepper

1 cup [230 g] whole-milk ricotta cheese

Stir together the warm water, yeast, and sugar in a mixer bowl and let stand for 5 minutes, or until creamy.

Using the paddle attachment on a stand mixer, beat in 3 Tbsp of the olive oil, 1½ tsp salt, half of the lemon zest, and the flour on low speed, or mix with a wooden spoon until a dough forms. Switch to the dough hook and knead on low speed for 2 to 3 minutes, or until the dough is smooth and elastic. If mixing by hand, turn the dough out onto a lightly floured work surface and knead with your hands for 3 to 4 minutes, or until the dough is soft, smooth, and still slightly sticky. (Add flour, 1 Tbsp at a time, if the dough is too sticky, but you want it to be soft and slightly sticky.)

Transfer the dough to a clean bowl and cover with plastic wrap. Let rise in a warm place for about 1½ hours, or until doubled.

Lightly oil a baking sheet. Punch down the dough and, using wet fingers, press it evenly on the prepared baking sheet into a rectangle about 10 by 12 in [25 by 30.5 cm]. Cover with a kitchen towel and let rise in a warm place for about 1 hour, or until doubled.

continued

If you have a baking stone, place it on the lower rack of the oven, and preheat the oven to 425°F [220°C].

Spread half of the pesto over the dough and drizzle with the remaining 2 Tbsp olive oil. Sprinkle with a little salt and pepper. Bake for about 20 minutes, or until the bread is lightly golden.

Meanwhile, combine the ricotta, lemon juice, and remaining lemon zest in a small bowl and season with salt and pepper.

Remove the bread from the oven and spread the remaining pesto over the top. (The first layer of pesto bakes in and the second layer gives the bread zip.) Dollop the ricotta mixture on top in 1-Tbsp drops. Return the bread to the oven for another 5 minutes.

Let cool on the baking sheet on a wire rack for 5 minutes, then cut into squares and serve warm or at room temperature. This bread is best served warm from the oven.

MAKES ONE 10-BY-12-IN [25-BY-30.5-CM] FLAT BREAD

FOUGASSE
WITH PRESERVED LEMON AND OLIVES

1⅔ cups [400 ml] warm (105°
to 115°F [40° to 45°C]) water

Scant 1 Tbsp active dry yeast

2 tsp sugar

4 cups [480 g] unbleached
all-purpose flour

Zest of 2 lemons

1½ tsp kosher salt

4 Tbsp [60 ml] extra-virgin
olive oil

½ cup [115 g] diced Preserved
Lemon (page 165), rinsed

About 20 Niçoise or
10 Kalamata olives, pitted

Coarse sea salt or sel gris
for sprinkling

Start to finish: 3 hours
Hands-on time: 45 minutes

Fougasse is a pretty flat bread from
Provence, with elongated holes that give
the bread the appearance of a leaf. I like to
use it as a rustic pizza, topping it here with
sunny preserved lemon and salty olives.

Stir together the warm water, yeast, and sugar in a mixer
bowl and let stand for about 5 minutes, or until creamy.

Using the paddle attachment on a stand mixer, beat
in 1 cup [120 g] of the flour, half of the lemon zest, the
kosher salt, and 2 Tbsp of the olive oil on low speed until
blended, or mix with a wooden spoon. Add half of the
preserved lemon and the remaining flour, 1 cup [120 g]
at a time, to form a slightly sticky dough. Switch to the
dough hook and knead on low speed for 2 to 3 minutes, or
until the dough is smooth and elastic. If mixing by hand,
turn the dough out onto a lightly floured work surface
and knead with your hands for 3 to 4 minutes, or until the
dough is soft, smooth, and still slightly sticky. (Add flour,
1 Tbsp at a time, if the dough is too sticky, but you want it
to be soft and slightly sticky.)

Transfer the dough to a clean bowl and cover with plastic wrap. Let rise in a warm place for about 1½ hours, or
until doubled.

ZESTY TIP

The dough can be made up to 1 day ahead.
After the first rise, refrigerate the dough,
still covered with plastic wrap. Bring to
room temperature before shaping and
then proceed as directed.

continued

Preheat the oven to 450°F [230°C].

Combine the remaining lemon zest and remaining 2 Tbsp olive oil in a small bowl.

Brush two baking sheets with some of the lemony olive oil. Divide the dough in half and, using wet or oiled hands, press out each half on a prepared baking sheet to form a rough oval. Stud the dough with the olives and remaining preserved lemon, and brush with the remaining lemony olive oil. Using a sharp knife, cut the dough down the center, then cut diagonal slits through the dough 2 to 3 in [5 to 7.5 cm] apart on both the left and right sides, leaving about a 1-in [2.5-cm] strip of dough between each and around the perimeter to form a leaf-like pattern. Pull the dough apart at the openings to show the bottom of the pan. Sprinkle with sea salt and let rise in a warm place for 20 minutes.

Bake for about 15 minutes, or until the bread is golden brown and slightly crispy on the bottom. Let cool on the baking sheet on wire racks for a few minutes before cutting. Serve warm or at room temperature. This bread is best eaten within 2 hours of baking.

SERVES 8

CREAM CHEESE MUFFINS
WITH SPINACH AND LEMON

Start to finish: 1 hour
Hands-on time: 30 minutes

My kids called these "spinach bombs" the first time I made them. The cream cheese gives the muffins a creamy density, and all that good green spinach is lightened up with lemon and a sprinkling of Parmesan cheese. Serve alongside a simple soup like chicken barley or tomato. Boom!

2 cups [240 g] unbleached all-purpose flour

2 tsp baking powder

¼ tsp baking soda

1 tsp kosher salt

1 cup [220 g] thawed frozen spinach, squeezed dry

4 oz [115 g] cream cheese, softened

2 large eggs

Zest of 2 lemons, plus 2 Tbsp fresh lemon juice

¾ cup [180 ml] buttermilk

¼ cup [60 ml] olive oil

¼ cup [20 g] grated Parmesan cheese

Preheat the oven to 350°F [180°C]. Grease a 12-cup muffin pan or line with paper cups.

Whisk the flour, baking powder, baking soda, and salt in a medium bowl until combined. Set aside.

Combine the spinach and cream cheese in a large bowl, and mash with a fork until no big lumps of cheese remain. Add the eggs, one at a time, mixing with the fork or a wooden spoon until incorporated. Mix in the lemon zest, lemon juice, buttermilk, and olive oil. Add the flour mixture all at once and stir with a wooden spoon just until mixed (don't overmix or the muffins will be tough).

Scoop the batter into the prepared muffin cups, filling them about three-fourths full. Sprinkle the tops with the Parmesan. Bake for 20 to 25 minutes, or until the tops spring back when pressed lightly. Let cool in the pan on a wire rack for 5 minutes, then turn out and serve warm. The muffins are best served within 2 hours of baking.

MAKES 12 MUFFINS

PARMESAN, LEMON, AND ROSEMARY MINI MUFFINS

1 cup [80 g] grated Parmesan cheese

1 cup [120 g] unbleached all-purpose flour

½ cup [70 g] cornmeal

1 Tbsp minced fresh rosemary

Zest of 2 lemons, plus 1 Tbsp fresh lemon juice

2 tsp baking powder

1 tsp sugar

¾ tsp kosher salt

½ tsp freshly ground pepper

¼ tsp baking soda

¾ cup [180 ml] buttermilk

2 large eggs

½ cup [120 ml] extra-virgin olive oil

Start to finish: 30 minutes
Hands-on time: 15 minutes

When soup-and-stew weather looms, it's handy to have a couple of quick and easy breads in mind to go with all that liquid soul food. Consider this a soul muffin. Yes, it might be a little cheesy, but the Parmesan, lemon, and extra-virgin olive oil in these savory nuggets make these mini bites a match for almost any recipe in your repertoire. Crumble them in or eat them on the side; these are the soul man of muffins. They really go with just about everything.

Preheat the oven to 350°F [180°C]. Line three 12-cup mini muffin pans with mini paper cups.

Whisk ¾ cup [60 g] of the Parmesan, the flour, cornmeal, rosemary, lemon zest, baking powder, sugar, salt, pepper, and baking soda in a large bowl until combined. Set aside.

Whisk the buttermilk, eggs, olive oil, and lemon juice in a medium bowl until blended. Add to the flour mixture and stir just until mixed (do not overmix).

Using a 1-Tbsp scoop, divide the batter among the prepared muffin cups. Sprinkle the tops with the remaining ¼ cup [20 g] Parmesan, distributing evenly among the muffins. Bake for about 15 minutes, or until firm to the touch. Let cool in the pans on wire racks for 5 minutes, then turn out and serve warm or at room temperature.

MAKES ABOUT 36 MINI MUFFINS

ZESTY TIP
Though best served the day they are made, the muffins can be stored, covered, in the freezer for up to 2 weeks. Thaw at room temperature and reheat briefly in a 300°F [150°C] oven.

TYROPITA

Start to finish:
2 hours, 15 minutes
Hands-on time: 45 minutes

Tyropita is a simple and delicious lemony cheese pie. You may have tried it as an appetizer shaped like a little turnover, made with buttery layers of phyllo. I made thousands of these as a caterer, but now prefer the timesaving but no less delicious way of layering everything in a pan and cutting it into triangles. I'll bet you can't eat just one piece.

ZESTY TIP

Once the *tyropita* is baked, it is difficult to reheat and will become soggy. The *tyropita* can be assembled before baking, covered, and refrigerated for up to 8 hours, or frozen for up to 1 month. Thaw in the refrigerator for 24 hours, then bake as directed.

6 Tbsp [85 g] unsalted butter, plus ½ cup [110 g], melted

⅓ cup [40 g] unbleached all-purpose flour

⅓ cup [80 ml] whole milk, warmed to lukewarm

½ tsp kosher salt

Dash of freshly grated nutmeg

Freshly ground pepper

4 large eggs, beaten

8 oz [230 g] feta cheese, crumbled

1 cup [80 g] grated kefalotiri or Parmesan cheese

1 cup [230 g] crumbled anthotiri or ricotta cheese

Zest of 2 lemons, plus 2 Tbsp fresh lemon juice

¼ cup [7 g] minced fresh flat-leaf parsley

8 oz [230 g] phyllo, thawed

Melt the 6 Tbsp [85 g] butter in a medium saucepan over medium heat. Add the flour and stir until the mixture becomes foamy. Whisk in the warm milk and cook for about 2 minutes, or until the white sauce is thickened and velvety. Remove from the heat. Stir in the salt, nutmeg, and pepper. Let cool for 5 minutes, then add the eggs, whisking them in one at a time. Stir in the feta, kefalotiri, anthotiri, lemon zest, lemon juice, and parsley. Set aside.

Preheat the oven to 350°F [180°C]. Butter a 9-by-13-in [23-by-33-cm] baking pan.

Remove the phyllo from its wrapper and cover it with a large sheet of plastic wrap topped by a damp dish towel. (Keep the pastry covered when not working with it to prevent air from drying it out.) Trim the phyllo sheets so they will fit in the bottom of the pan without overlapping the sides.

sweet and tart

To build the *tyropita*, you will alternate three layers of dough with two layers of the cheese mixture. Start with a base of six sheets of phyllo on the bottom, brushing the top of each sheet with some of the melted butter. Spread half of the cheese mixture evenly over the stacked sheets and press lightly. Cover with another three sheets of phyllo, again brushing the top of each with melted butter, then spread the remaining cheese mixture over the sheets. Top with another six sheets of phyllo, brushing each with butter the same way. (Refrigerate remaining phyllo, tightly wrapped in plastic, for up to 3 days; do not refreeze.)

If you have the time, cover and refrigerate the tyropita for 30 minutes so the butter sets (this will make the tyropita easier to cut after baking because the pastry becomes very flaky). Using a sharp knife, make six to eight cuts on the diagonal lengthwise through the top few layers of pastry, then cut diagonally from the opposite direction to form diamonds. Bake for about 45 minutes, or until golden and flaky. Remove from the oven and, following the cuts already made, cut completely through the *tyropita*. Serve warm or at room temperature.

MAKES ABOUT 32 PIECES

151
savories

SUMMER TART
WITH LEMON AND SUN-DRIED TOMATOES

Start to finish: 1 hour
Hands-on time: 25 minutes

It's valuable to have an easy-to-make appetizer in your repertoire that looks much more impressive than it has any right to be. This is that appetizer. Purchased puff pastry all dolled up with lemony cheese and sun-dried tomatoes comes together (almost) effortlessly and satisfies deliciously.

ZESTY TIPS

Boursin is a triple-cream cheese flavored with herbs and pepper. It's a time-saver because it carries the herbal notes through this tart without having to cut and add herbs to the dish.

The tarts can be completely assembled before baking, covered, and frozen for up to 4 weeks. Thaw at room temperature for 1 hour, then bake as directed. The filling can be mixed and stored, covered, in the refrigerator for up to 2 days.

One 17.3-oz [490-g] package frozen puff pastry (2 sheets), thawed

2 egg yolks, beaten

5 oz [140 g] Boursin or other herbed soft cheese, softened

4 oz [115 g] goat cheese, softened

¼ cup [20 g] grated Parmesan cheese

Zest of 1 lemon, plus 2 tsp fresh lemon juice

Freshly ground pepper

½ cup [100 g] sun-dried tomatoes packed in oil, drained and julienned

Preheat the oven to 425°F [220°C]. Line two baking sheets with parchment paper.

On a lightly floured work surface, roll out one sheet of puff pastry into an 11-by-14-in [28-by-35.5-cm] rectangle. Transfer to one of the prepared baking sheets and cut 1-in [2.5-cm] strips off of each side, reserving the strips. Brush the edges of the rectangle with water and fit the strips on the edges, creating a border. Poke holes all over the bottom of the pastry with a fork. Repeat with the remaining pastry sheet. Bake for about 10 minutes, or until puffy and brown. Remove from the oven and poke again with a fork. Gently push the pastry down as it will be puffy and raised. Return to the oven and bake for another 5 minutes. Let cool completely on the baking sheets on wire racks.

Turn the oven temperature to 350°F [180°C].

Combine the egg yolks, Boursin, goat cheese, Parmesan, lemon zest, and lemon juice in a medium bowl and season with pepper. Mix with a fork until well combined. Spread the mixture over the cooled pastries and top with the sun-dried tomatoes. Bake for about 20 minutes, or until the cheese is set. Let cool on the baking sheets on wire racks for 10 minutes before cutting into squares and serving.

MAKES 2 TARTS

LEMONY PESTO—GOAT CHEESE DIP
WITH VEGETABLES

Start to finish: 20 minutes
Hands-on time: 20 minutes

Tangy goat cheese is a natural with lemon and pesto. And who doesn't love goat cheese? I've come to rely on this creamy dip more often than I care to admit.

⅓ cup [45 g] pine nuts

8 oz [230 g] goat cheese, softened

½ cup [120 ml] plain whole-milk Greek yogurt

2 Tbsp Lemony Basil Pesto (page 164)

Zest and juice of 1 lemon

½ cup [100 g] diced roasted red bell pepper

Assorted raw vegetables for serving, such as carrots, celery, fennel, broccoli, and red and yellow bell pepper strips

Lemon, Pepper, and Asiago Crackers (page 140) or your favorite store-bought crackers for serving

In a microwave-safe bowl, toast the pine nuts for 30 seconds. Stir and microwave for another 30 seconds. Stir again and if the nuts aren't oily and fragrant, microwave for another 30 seconds. Let cool. Alternatively, toast the nuts in a skillet over medium heat, tossing them every now and then, until toasted, about 3 minutes.

Combine the goat cheese, yogurt, pesto, lemon zest, and lemon juice in the bowl of a food processor and process until well blended. Alternatively, combine the ingredients in a large bowl and stir with a fork. (Add more yogurt to thin the dip, if desired.) Store, covered, in the refrigerator for up to 2 days.

Transfer the dip to a serving bowl, and top with the roasted red bell pepper and toasted pine nuts. Serve with the vegetables and crackers.

MAKES ABOUT 1½ CUPS [425 G]

CHAPTER 7
BASICS

The dishes in this chapter will take your citrus love to another level. You may live an entire life without making candied lemon peel or preserved lemons, but life is definitely sweeter if you make time to whip up a batch.

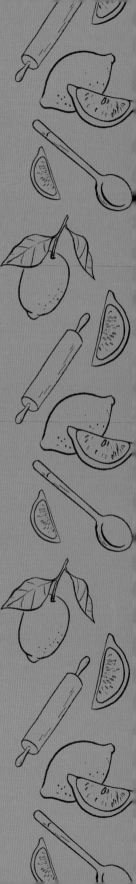

LEMON CURD

¾ cup [180 ml] fresh lemon juice, plus zest of 2 lemons

1¼ cups [250 g] sugar

1 cup [220 g] unsalted butter, cubed

5 large eggs, plus 2 egg yolks

Pinch of kosher salt

There are few citrusy desserts as lemony as lemon curd. It's the magic bullet of lemon tartness and will shoot that zesty, tangy flavor into biscuits, trifles, and cake fillings, or can be combined with whipped cream, ricotta, or mascarpone to fill éclairs, cupcakes, and crêpes.

ZESTY TIP

When cooking lemon curd or any type of eggy curd, stir constantly with a heat-proof rubber spatula or wooden spoon. The wide bottom keeps the curd moving, minimizing the chance of it scrambling.

Combine the lemon juice, sugar, and butter in a medium saucepan over medium heat and bring to a boil, stirring occasionally.

Whisk the eggs, egg yolks, and salt in a medium heat-proof bowl until combined. While whisking rapidly, slowly pour in the hot lemon juice mixture. Return the egg mixture to the saucepan and cook over medium heat, stirring constantly with a heat-proof spatula, for 2 to 3 minutes, or until slightly thickened. Do not boil or the eggs will curdle. The lemon curd should coat the back of the spatula. It will thicken further as it cools.

Immediately transfer the lemon curd to a heat-proof bowl (it will continue to cook in the hot pan and could scramble) and stir in the lemon zest. Continue stirring for 1 minute to cool, then let cool to room temperature. Store, covered, in the refrigerator for up to 3 days.

MAKES ABOUT 2½ CUPS [700 G]

ORANGE CURD

1 cup [240 ml] fresh orange juice, plus zest of 2 oranges, preferably Valencia or navel oranges

1 cup [200 g] sugar

½ cup [110 g] unsalted butter, cubed

2 large eggs, plus 6 egg yolks

Pinch of kosher salt

Start to finish: 20 minutes
Hands-on time: 20 minutes

Combine the orange juice, sugar, and butter in a medium saucepan over medium heat and bring to a boil, stirring occasionally.

Whisk the eggs, egg yolks, and salt in a medium heat-proof bowl until combined. While whisking rapidly, slowly pour in the hot orange juice mixture. Return the egg mixture to the saucepan and cook over medium heat, stirring constantly with a heat-proof spatula, for 2 to 3 minutes, or until slightly thickened. Do not boil or the eggs will curdle. The orange curd should coat the back of the spatula. It will thicken further as it cools.

Immediately transfer the orange curd to a heat-proof bowl (it will continue to cook in the hot pan and could scramble) and stir in the orange zest. Continue stirring for 1 minute to cool, then let cool to room temperature. Store, covered, in the refrigerator for up to 3 days.

MAKES ABOUT 2 CUPS [560 G]

Orange curd is just as delicious as lemon curd, though not quite as tart. You can use it in the same way as its lemon cousin when you'd like an orange rather than a lemon accent.

ZESTY TIP

Use thin-skinned oranges for the best juice yield.

LEMON MARMALADE

Start to finish: 2 hours
Hands-on time: 1 hour

Most of us are familiar with orange marmalade, but lemon marmalade is equally charming. It isn't hard to make a batch, fitting it in between other things during the course of a day. The reason you should make it is a revelation: Spread over toast or English muffins, this marmalade is truly a sunny way to begin the day.

9 lemons, scrubbed

6 cups [1.4 L] water

6 cups [1.2 kg] sugar

Cut the pointy ends off the lemons and cut each lemon in half lengthwise, then cut each half lengthwise into three wedges. Remove the seeds and cut out the pesky white membrane that runs through the core of the lemon. Reserve the seeds and membranes and tie them up in a cheesecloth bag (they will add pectin to help thicken the marmalade).

Using a very sharp knife, cut the wedges crosswise into thin little triangles. Transfer to a large nonreactive (not aluminum) wide pot. Pour in the water, add the cheese-cloth bag, and bring to a boil over medium-high heat. Turn the heat to low and simmer for about 30 minutes, or until the lemons are soft. Remove the bag and discard.

Chill a small plate in the freezer.

Stir the sugar into the pot and return to a boil over medium-high heat. Turn the heat to low and boil the marmalade for about 30 minutes, or until a candy thermometer reads 220°F [104°C.] Make sure that the thermometer is suspended in the fruit and does not touch the bottom of the pan. Drop about ¼ tsp marmalade onto the chilled plate and let it cool for a moment. Push the edge of it with your finger; if it wrinkles and has thickened, the marmalade is ready. If not, continue to boil for another 5 minutes and test again.

continued

Sterilize six 1-cup [240-ml] jars and lids in boiling water. Fill the hot jars with hot marmalade to within ¼ in [6 mm] of the top. Wipe the top edge of the jars clean with a damp cloth. Working quickly, screw on the lids (be careful, they are hot) and set the jars aside to cool on your kitchen counter overnight. The tops should make a tight seal as they cool. If a few don't seal (the top will push down and click when pressed), refrigerate and use within a month or so. The marmalade will disappear more quickly than you think. Store, unopened, at room temperature for up to 1 year. Refrigerate opened jars for up to 3 months.

MAKES SIX 1-CUP [240-ML] JARS

162

sweet and tart

LEMON SYRUP
WITH LEMONGRASS

½ cup [100 g] sugar

½ cup [120 ml] water

1 strip lemon peel, plus 3 Tbsp fresh lemon juice

2 stalks lemongrass, bulb or white part only, smashed

2 Tbsp rum

Start to finish: 40 minutes

Hands-on time: 10 minutes

Combine the sugar, water, lemon peel, lemon juice, and lemongrass in a medium saucepan over medium heat and bring to a simmer. Boil for 10 minutes, or until slightly thickened. Let cool for about 30 minutes to allow the flavors to deepen, then stir in the rum. Pour the syrup through a fine-mesh strainer into a small container. Store, covered, in the refrigerator for up to 2 weeks.

MAKES ABOUT 1 CUP [240 ML]

A good lemon syrup is a fine thing to have on hand. I love this one for lemony cocktails, mixed with a little fresh fruit, or brushed over layer cakes and pound cakes. The lemongrass lends an addictive floral note and makes whatever you toss the syrup with just a little more sophisticated.

LEMONY BASIL PESTO

Start to finish: 20 minutes

Hands-on time: 20 minutes

I often refer to pesto as "summer in a jar." Whenever I see a nice big bunch of fresh basil leaves at the grocery store, you can be sure that pesto will soon be in my freezer. It's wonderful in warmer months, but there's something about that little blast of summer during bleak winter days that really brightens my world. This lemony version just shouts "party!" I hope you like it as much as I do. It's delicious spread on crostini for an easy appetizer, or added to soups and stews.

2 garlic cloves

1 cup [120 g] walnuts

Kosher salt

Zest of 2 lemons, plus 2 Tbsp fresh lemon juice

3 cups [90 g] fresh basil leaves, stemmed

½ cup [120 ml] extra-virgin olive oil, plus more for drizzling

1 cup [80 g] grated Parmesan cheese

Freshly ground pepper

Drop the garlic into the bowl of a food processor while the processor is running. Turn off the machine, add the walnuts and 1 tsp salt, and pulse until finely ground. Add the lemon zest and basil and pulse until still a little chunky. Add the olive oil, lemon juice, and Parmesan and season with pepper. Pulse again until the desired texture is reached (I like my pesto a little coarse). Taste and adjust the seasoning if necessary with salt and pepper.

Transfer to storage containers and drizzle over a little olive oil to keep the pesto green. Store in the refrigerator for up to 2 weeks, or freeze for up to 3 months.

MAKES ABOUT 1½ CUPS [360 ML]

PRESERVED LEMONS

6 lemons, preferably organic   ⅓ cup [70 g] kosher salt

Trim the stem ends and cut each lemon into six wedges. Toss with the salt in a large bowl. Pack the lemons into two 1-pt [480-ml] jars, sprinkling in the extra salt from the bowl and pressing down on them to extract juice as you go. Make sure that the lemon wedges on top are covered with juice. (You may need to squeeze the juice from another lemon or two and add the juice to the jars.) Seal each jar with a lid and store in a cool, dark place for 1 month, shaking the jars once or twice a day.

Store, unopened, at room temperature for up to 1 year. Refrigerate opened jars for up to 6 months; be sure to keep the lemon wedges submerged in the salty lemon juice or mold may grow.

MAKES 36 LEMON WEDGES

Whole lemons break down during a month of curing in salt and lemon juice, yielding these salty-velvety citrus wedges that are definitely worth the wait. Rinse the lemons well under running cold water before using them in stews, braises, couscous and salads, and as a topping for breads and pizzas.

165
basics

CANDIED LEMON SLICES

Start to finish: 2 days
Hands-on time: 30 minutes

3 lemons, preferably Meyer, sliced (see Zesty Tip)

1½ cups [300 g] sugar

1 cup [240 ml] water

You can candy any variety of lemon, but Meyer lemons are an especially pretty color. I like to use these as a garnish on lemon desserts . . . or just eat them out of hand. Or dip in chocolate as directed for Chocolate-Dipped Candied Citrus Peel (facing page).

Put the lemon slices in a medium saucepan and add water to cover. Bring to a boil over medium-high heat. Boil for 5 minutes, then drain and transfer the lemons to a bowl.

Combine the sugar and the 1 cup [240 ml] water in the same pan over medium-high heat and bring to a boil, stirring occasionally. Once the sugar is dissolved, add the drained lemons and bring to a simmer. Turn the heat to low and simmer the lemons for about 1 hour, or until translucent. Remove from the heat. Set a large strainer over a medium bowl and drain the lemons. (Reserve the syrup for another use.)

ZESTY TIPS

Use the leftover sugar syrup to make cocktails, flavor iced tea, or brush between cake layers.

How you slice the lemons is important. Too thin and they will disintegrate; too thick and they will be unpleasantly chewy and clunky. Cut off the pointy ends so that you can see the flesh, then cut the lemons crosswise into slices about ⅛ in [4 mm] thick. All of them won't be pretty but that's okay (you can just eat those first).

Coat a wire rack with nonstick cooking spray and place on a baking sheet. Arrange the lemon slices in a single layer on the rack. Let dry overnight. If they are still somewhat sticky, continue to air-dry for another day. Store in an airtight container, separating the layers with parchment paper, at room temperature for up to 4 weeks.

MAKES ABOUT 20 SLICES

CHOCOLATE-DIPPED CANDIED CITRUS PEEL

3 lemons, 2 oranges, or
1 grapefruit

2 cups [400 g] sugar

1½ cups [360 ml] water

6 oz [170 g] high-quality white
or dark chocolate, chopped
into small pieces

Start to finish: 24 hours
Hands-on time: 1 hour

Coat a wire rack with nonstick cooking spray and place on a baking sheet. Line another baking sheet with parchment paper.

Make four slits along the length of each citrus fruit from end to end, cutting through the peel but not into the flesh. Using your fingers, gently peel the skin from the fruit and reserve the fruit for another use. Cut the peel into thin strips, about ¼ in [6 mm] wide.

Put the peel in a medium saucepan and add water to cover. Bring to a boil over medium-high heat, turn the heat to low, and simmer for 15 minutes. Drain, cover with fresh water, and repeat the process. Drain and rinse the peel.

Combine 1½ cups [300 g] of the sugar and the 1½ cups [360 ml] water in the same pan over medium-high heat and bring to a boil, stirring occasionally. Once the sugar is dissolved, add the drained peel, turn the heat to low, and simmer for about 40 minutes, or until the peel is very tender and looks translucent.

Scoop the peel from the syrup with a fork and arrange in a single layer on the prepared rack. Let dry for about 30 minutes, then dredge the peel in the remaining ½ cup [100 g] sugar in a shallow bowl (this helps to prevent the peel strips from sticking to each other). Place the peel in a single layer on the parchment-lined baking sheet and let dry overnight.

Sure, candied citrus is delicious, but candied citrus with chocolate . . . now you're speaking my language.

And sure, you can buy candied citrus peel. But it will never be as good as the ones you can make at home. These little citrus strips make a perfect ending to a meal when served with shortbread cookies and strong coffee. But they are just as good diced into biscotti or used as a garnish on a simple lemon cake.

ZESTY TIP

Tempering your chocolate will allow it to firm up at room temperature. It will also be shinier and prettier.

continued

167
basics

Melt 5 oz [140 g] of the chocolate in a stainless-steel bowl set over a pan of simmering water; be sure that the bottom of the bowl doesn't touch the water. Don't walk away from it; just stand there and stir. When the chocolate is half melted, remove the bowl from the pan of water and continue to stir on the countertop. It will begin to cool but the chocolate will continue to melt. Once completely melted, stir in the remaining 1 oz [30 g] chocolate, then continue stirring gently until the chocolate is cool and no longer melts. Remove any unmelted pieces.

Line another baking sheet with parchment paper. Dip the peel strips halfway into the chocolate and arrange in a single layer on the second prepared baking sheet. Let stand for about 1 hour, or until the chocolate is firm. Store in an airtight container, separating the layers with parchment paper, at room temperature for up to 3 weeks.

MAKES ABOUT 60 PIECES

FLAKY PASTRY

Start to finish:
1 hour, 10 minutes
Hands-on time: 20 minutes

3 cups [360 g] all-purpose flour

½ tsp kosher salt

1¼ cups [275 g] cold unsalted butter, cubed

⅔ cup [160 ml] ice water

Homemade pastry is easy when you have a good recipe and understand a few of the dynamics. I've been assembling it in my food processor for more than twenty years, and this is still the easiest way I know to create delicious pie dough. Practice does make perfect, so get busy and make a few batches when you have a little time. Your inner kitchen goddess (or god) will be smiling that knowing smile that says, "But of course I can whip up a ravishing dessert at a moment's notice. Can't everyone do that?"

ZESTY TIP

For the best results, I like to freeze all the ingredients to make them super-cold. That way, the food-processor motor doesn't overheat the butter, making it harder to work with. Bringing the dough together with your hands will ensure it doesn't get overworked in the processor. The idea is to leave tiny bits of butter that are suspended in the dough and then melt as the pastry bakes, creating that flaky texture we all love.

Combine the flour, salt, and butter in a medium bowl or on a piece of plastic wrap and place in the freezer for at least 30 minutes, or up to 1 hour.

Remove from the freezer and put the flour mixture in the bowl of a food processor. Pulse ten to fifteen times to cut the butter into the flour. Quickly pour the ice water through the feed tube while pulsing another ten to fifteen times. The dough will still look shaggy and rough (to achieve a tender, flaky pastry, don't overprocess at this point). Turn the pastry out onto a lightly floured work surface, divide it equally into two portions, and compress each into a disk with your hands. You may have to knead the dough lightly with the heel of your hand to bring it together. Wrap in plastic wrap and refrigerate for about 30 minutes (this will make it easier to roll out).

When ready to roll out the dough, lightly flour a work surface, place the unwrapped disk of dough on the flour, and lightly dust the top of the disk with more flour. Pound the dough with a rolling pin to soften it slightly and then roll the dough gently but firmly, picking it up after each roll and rotating it from twelve o'clock to three o'clock. (Rotating the dough keeps it from sticking and helps to maintain a round shape.) Dust the work surface with more flour if necessary to prevent sticking.

sweet and tart

When you have rolled the dough to the desired size and thickness (typically about 16 in [40.5 cm] round and ⅛ in [4 mm] thick), fold the dough in half and then in half again to prevent it from tearing while moving it to the pie plate. Unfold the dough and use as directed in the recipe.

Even if you aren't going to use the other disk of pastry right away, I recommend that you roll it out the same way, place it on a parchment-lined baking sheet, and freeze it. Once firm, transfer it from the baking sheet, wrap it in the parchment and plastic wrap, and store in the freezer for up to 3 months. To use, thaw in the refrigerator overnight, or at room temperature for about 30 minutes. It is ready to use when it becomes pliable and easily fits into your pie plate.

MAKES TWO 9-IN [23-CM] SHELLS

Acknowledgments

✳ ✳ ✳

Thank you to the extraordinary people at Chronicle Books for creating the most beautiful cookbooks in the business. I send much affection and gratitude to my editor, Bill LeBlond, for his vision of this book, to editor par excellence (and fellow Pittsburgher) Sarah Billingsley and managing editor Doug Ogan for polishing the manuscript till it sparkled, and to copyeditor Kris Balloun for her tireless attention to detail. *Mille mercis* to art director Vanessa Dina, photographer Nicole Franzen, prop stylist Kate Jordan, and food stylist Chelsea Zimmer for the gorgeous design and photography and for creating a lighthearted, easy-to-read book to be proud of for many years to come. Kudos to Tera Killip and Steve Kim for getting the book ready for the printer, and to marketing manager Peter Perez and publicist David Hawk for packaging and promoting *Sweet and Tart* to the masses.

Kisses and hugs to John McMillan and the Bun Babes at Great Lakes Baking Company, and especially to Cam, who more than filled my shoes and became a local cookie superstar.

With appreciation to my countless students and friends who've recipe tested and critiqued over the years: Julie Neri, Mary Lohman, Sarah McNally, Brigitte Gottfried, Anne Pitkin, Tammy Karasek, Terri Thompson, Sarina Kinney, Mary Anne Kickel, Maria Isabella, Ann Richardson, Anne Gallagher, Elsa de Cardenas, Janet Redman, Gayle Joyce, Mickey Shankland, Kathy Belden, Beth Balzarini, Jamie Stevens, Sue Koob, Barb VanBlarcum, Laura Micco, John and Kim LaScola, Elaine George, Angela and Terry Gagel, Kelly Ross Brown, Camerin Winovich, Connie Sandberg, and Dave McIlvaine. Thanks for buying all those lemons when they were $1 apiece.

Special thanks to my kids Jessica, Justin, and Corey; daughters-in-law Lyndsey and Sara; and son-in-law JR for always lending a helpful hand at family dinners and get-togethers. Whether it's making pasta, setting the table, or doing the dishes, my best days are spent in the kitchen with you.

And last but not least, to my loving husband, Rick, who, though he loves sweet things, tries very hard not to eat them. Thanks for tasting (almost) everything.

INDEX